mathematics

FOR LEARNING

The Box Factory

Extending Multiplication with the Array

Miki Jensen

Catherine Twomey Fosnot

Heinemann

DEDICATED TO TEACHERS™

361 Hanover Street
Portsmouth, NH 03801–3912
firsthand.heinemann.com

Offices and agents throughout the world

ISBN 13: 978-0-325-01020-5
ISBN 10: 0-325-01020-X

ISBN 13: 978-0-15-360572-7
ISBN 10: 0-15-360572-3

 The development of a portion of the material described within was supported in part by the National Science Foundation under Grant No. 9911841. Any opinions, findings, and conclusions or recommendations expressed in these materials are those of the authors and do not necessarily reflect the views of the National Science Foundation.

Library of Congress Cataloging-in-Publication Data
CIP data is on file with the Library of Congress

Printed in the United States of America on acid-free paper

21 20 19   GP   6   7

Acknowledgements

Photography

Herbert Seignoret
Mathematics in the City, City College of New York

Illustrator

Bandelin-Dacey

Schools featured in photographs
The Muscota New School/PS 314 (an empowerment school in Region 10), New York, NY
Independence School/PS 234 (Region 9), New York, NY
Fort River Elementary School, Amherst, MA

Contents

Unit Overview

The focus of this unit is the deepening and extending of students' understanding of multiplication, specifically the associative and commutative properties and their use with computation, systematic factoring, and the extension of students' understanding of two-dimensional rectangular arrays to three-dimensional arrays within rectangular prisms.

The unit includes a series of investigations based on the context of a cardboard box factory. Initially students design a variety of boxes (rectangular prisms) that hold 24 items arranged in rows, columns, and layers. The questions posed in the first investigation (how many box arrangements are possible, and how do we know for certain that we have found all the possibilities) give students an opportunity to explore the associative and commutative properties, factor pairs, doubling and halving strategies, and systematic ways of organizing their work to determine all possible cases. In the second and third investigations, students analyze the amount and cost of

The Landscape of Learning

BIG IDEAS

- The commutative property of multiplication
- The place value patterns that occur when multiplying by the base
- The associative property of multiplication
- The dimensions of length and width can be used to produce a square unit measurement of area for rectangles
- The dimensions of length, width, and height can be used to produce a cubic unit measurement of volume for rectangular solids
- The surface area of rectangular solids increases as the measures of the three dimensions (length, width, height) diverge
- Doubling each dimension of a rectangular solid results in a new solid, with a volume that is 2^3 times the volume of the original solid

STRATEGIES

- Using repeated addition
- Skip-counting
- Using partial products
- Using ten-times
- Doubling and halving
- Factoring and grouping flexibly

MODEL

- Open array

the cardboard needed for their boxes, deepening their understanding of the associative property, examining congruency vs. equivalency, and exploring the relationship of surface area to the shape of the box. Subsequent investigations involve using two different cubic boxes as units of measurement, and determining the volume of a shipping box that measures 4 feet by 6 feet by 4 feet. By the end of the unit, formulas for surface area and volume of rectangular prisms are the focus.

Several minilessons for multiplication are included in the unit as well—these are structured as strings of related problems explicitly designed to guide learners toward computational fluency with whole-number multiplication, by focusing on factors and efficient grouping.

The Mathematical Landscape

For multiplication and division, the array model can be a powerful tool. Partial products can be represented on it, and the relationship of these to the total area can be explored to develop an understanding of the distributive and commutative properties. Research by Battista et al. (1998), however, suggests that the array model is often difficult for learners to understand because the ability to coordinate rows and columns simultaneously requires a substantial cognitive reorganization—and thus an understanding of arrays develops through successive stages. The unit in this series that supports the early development of arrays is *Muffles' Truffles*. *The Box Factory* is to be used for later development as it assumes that your students have some previous knowledge of arrays. It is designed to support students as they develop a deeper understanding of the array, extending the model from two to three dimensions, and using it as a tool to examine the associative property for multiplication and the relationship of surface area to volume, for rectangular solids.

This unit is designed to encourage the development of some of the big ideas related to multiplication. These include:

❖ *the commutative property of multiplication*

❖ *the place value patterns that occur when multiplying by the base*

❖ *the associative property of multiplication*

❖ *the dimensions of length and width can be used to produce a square unit measurement of area for rectangles*

❖ *the dimensions of length, width, and height can be used to produce a cubic unit measurement of volume for rectangular solids*

❖ *the surface area of rectangular solids increases as the measures of the three dimensions (length, width, height) diverge*

❖ *doubling each dimension of a rectangular solid results in a new solid, with a volume that is 2^3 times the volume of the original solid*

❖ The commutative property of multiplication

Multiplication is commutative: $a \times b = b \times a$. Picture a rectangular array (drawn on graph paper) that measures 4 inches by 19 inches. If we turn this array 90 degrees, we have a 19×4 array. Using arrays like this is exactly what students do to convince each other of the commutative property. They often call it the turn-around rule. There are many opportunities in this unit for students to construct this big idea as they explore rectangular arrangements in rows and columns. They also investigate the surface area of the boxes they build and come to realize that no matter how the array is rotated, the area is the same.

❖ The place value patterns that occur when multiplying by the base

Precisely because multiplication is commutative, an interesting thing happens when we multiply by the base—the factor "bumps over" to the appropriate column. For example, $10 \times 4 = 4 + 4 + 4 + 4 + 4 + 4 + 4 + 4 + 4 + 4$. The result of 40 seems amazing to students, who often say that they added a zero or refer to the zero trick. The reason this "trick" works is that we can think of the 10 groups of four as 4 groups of ten—so the 4 is placed ("bumps over") into the tens place. It is important to support students in exploring why this pattern occurs—to help them construct how place value is involved.

❖ The associative property of multiplication

The associative property also holds for multiplication: (a × b) × c = a × (b × c). Picture a three-dimensional array (rows, columns, and layers)—perhaps an arrangement of oranges in a box. Imagine that each layer has 3 rows with 6 oranges in each and that there are 2 layers. This arrangement could be represented as (3 × 6) × 2. The box could be flipped and the oranges arranged in a layer that has 6 rows with 2 oranges in each. Now there are 3 layers, yet the total number of oranges remains the same: (3 × 6) × 2 = 3 × (6 × 2). There are many opportunities in this unit for students to construct this big idea as they explore three-dimensional arrangements in rows, columns, and layers.

❖ The dimensions of length and width can be used to produce a square unit measurement of area for rectangles

Counting objects in rows and columns is easier for students than understanding that the area covered can be measured in square units, the dimensions of which are determined by linear units used to measure length and width. For this reason, the unit begins with arrangements of objects in rows and columns, but soon students are asked to explore the surface area of boxes they are building for their arrangements and graph paper arrays are used to represent the area of the faces of the boxes.

❖ The dimensions of length, width, and height can be used to produce a cubic unit measurement of volume for rectangular solids

The measurement of three-dimensional space is even more difficult. Determining the characteristics of the cubic unit that is created can be quite challenging. As students explore and mathematize the situations in this unit, they will grapple with the problem of understanding how the measurements of the box dimensions can be used to determine the volume of the box.

❖ The surface area of rectangular solids increases as the measures of the three dimensions (length, width, height) diverge

In other words, for rectangular solids, the closer one gets to a cube, the smaller the amount of surface area. Often students assume that because volume is conserved when a box is transformed, the surface area stays the same, too. They are quite surprised to discover that the closer one gets to a cube when changing the dimensions (length, width, and height), the less surface area is exposed. In students' words, "there is more of the outside inside now."

❖ Doubling each dimension of a rectangular solid results in a new solid, with a volume that is 2^3 times the volume of the original solid

At first, students assume that because the dimensions doubled, the volume should double. As they build layers of the three-dimensional array and explore how the volume changes, and as they grapple to understand how the linear units of the dimensions interact multiplicatively to form the cubic units, they come to realize how volume increases.

STRATEGIES

As you work with the activities in this unit, you will notice that students will use many strategies to solve the problems that are posed to them. Here are some strategies to notice:

❖ *using repeated addition*

❖ *skip-counting*

❖ *using partial products*

❖ *using ten-times*

❖ *doubling and halving*

❖ *factoring and grouping flexibly*

Using repeated addition

Often the first strategy students use to solve multiplication problems is repeated addition. This is because they are viewing the situation additively, rather than multiplicatively. To solve 6×4 (how many oranges are in this one-layer box), students will write (or think about) $4 + 4 + 4 + 4 + 4 + 4$ and then add to find the total. Repeated addition should be seen as a starting place in the journey, but not as the end point. As you confer with students, you will need to help them to keep track of the groups, and you can encourage more efficient grouping (such as turning the 6 fours into pairs of fours, resulting in 3 eights).

Skip-counting

The struggle to keep track of the groups usually pushes students to skip-count. Although they are still thinking about the situation additively rather than multiplicatively, they keep track of the groups mentally and skip-count. To figure out how many oranges are in a 6×4 one-layer box, they might say 4, 8, 12, 16, 20, 24.

Using partial products

An important shift in multiplicative thinking occurs when students begin to make partial products—they use a fact they know to make another. For example, they might reason that a 3×4 box of oranges with 2 layers holds $(3 \times 4) + (3 \times 4)$ oranges. Or they might multiply 12×18 by using $(10 \times 18) + (2 \times 18)$. The big idea underlying this strategy is the distributive property.

Using ten-times

Once students begin to make use of partial products, an important strategy to encourage is the use of the ten-times partial product. This can be very helpful for dealing with larger numbers—for example, 12×30. It is helpful to think about this as $12 \times 3 \times 10$. Of course, this strategy is helpful only if students have constructed an understanding of the place value patterns that occur when multiplying by the base.

Doubling and halving

As students' multiplicative reasoning becomes stronger, they develop the ability to group more efficiently. They begin to realize that if they double the number of groups and want the total product to be the same, they need to halve the amount in each group: $4 \times 6 = 8 \times 3$.

Factoring and grouping flexibly

Doubling and halving can be generalized to tripling and thirding, or quadrupling and quartering, etc. The big idea underlying the reason these strategies work is the associative property of multiplication. In multiplication, the factors can be associated in a variety of ways that may make multiplication problems easy to do mentally. For example, $28 \times 5 = (14 \times 2) \times 5 = 14 \times (2 \times 5) = 140$. Efficient computation results when students realize that they can factor the factors and regroup them to make the computation easier.

MATHEMATICAL MODELING

The primary focus of this unit is the extension of a two-dimensional array model to the three-dimensional array model for multiplication. Initially the model is introduced as the arrangement of oranges in a box with multiple layers. Boxes are used to explore the associative property and the relationship of surface area to volume. Eventually cubic box units are used to generalize a formula for determining the volume of rectangular prisms.

The array is a powerful model for multiplicative thinking because it can support the development of the following:

- a wide range of strategies (skip-counting, repeated addition, doubling, doubling and halving, partial products) and big ideas like the distributive, associative, and commutative properties

- visual representations for what multiplication means (e.g., 6×8 can be understood as 6 rows of 8 squares or 8 columns of 6 squares)

- an understanding of area and perimeter, surface area, dimensions, and volume

Models go through three stages of development (Gravemeijer 1999; Fosnot and Dolk 2002):

- *model of the situation*

- *model of students' strategies*

- *model as a tool for thinking*

❖ Model of the situation

Initially models grow out of visually representing the situation. In this unit arrays are introduced in the context of an arrangement (rows, columns, and layers) of oranges in a box. As students explore a variety of box designs, graph paper arrays emerge as a representation of the faces of the box, and volume emerges as the number of cubic boxes that can fill a shipping box.

❖ Model of students' strategies

Students benefit from seeing the teacher model their strategies. Once a model has been introduced as a representation of the situation, you can use it to display student strategies. If a student says in solving $2\frac{1}{2} \times 24$, "I doubled and halved. I used 5×12, then 10×6," draw the following:

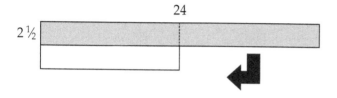

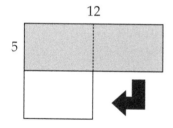

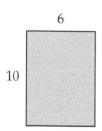

Representations like these give students a chance to discuss a variety of strategies.

❖ Model as a tool for thinking

Eventually students become able to use the array model as a tool to think with—to prove and explore their ideas about multiplicative reasoning. Here, as the dimensions of a box are visualized in relationship to other boxes, students can explore the associative property and explore changes in the fact that volume changes as the dimensions of the boxes change.

Many opportunities to discuss these landmarks in mathematical development will arise as you work through this unit. Look for moments of puzzlement. Don't hesitate to let students discuss their ideas and check and recheck their strategies. Celebrate their accomplishments! They are young mathematicians at work.

A graphic of the full landscape of learning for multiplication and division is provided on page 11. The purpose of the graphic is to allow you to see the longer journey of students' mathematical development and to place your work with this unit within the scope of this long-term development. You may also find the graphic helpful as a way to record the progress of individual students for yourself. Each landmark can be shaded in as you find evidence in a student's work and in what the student says—evidence that a landmark strategy, big idea, or way of modeling has been constructed. In a sense, you will be recording the individual pathways your students take as they develop as young mathematicians.

References and Resources

Battista, Michael T., Douglas H. Clements, Judy Arnoff, Kathryn Battista, and Caroline Auken Bomsn. 1998. Students' spatial structuring of 2D arrays of squares. *Journal for Research in Mathematics Education* 29:503–32.

Dolk, Maarten, and Catherine Twomey Fosnot. 2005a. *Fostering Children's Mathematical Development, Grades 3–5: The Landscape of Learning.* CD-ROM with accompanying facilitator's guide by Sherrin B. Hersch, Catherine Twomey Fosnot, and Antonia Cameron. Portsmouth, NH: Heinemann.

———. 2005b. *Multiplication and Division Minilessons, Grades 3–5.* CD-ROM with accompanying facilitator's guide by Antonia Cameron, Carol Mosesson Teig, Sherrin B. Hersch, and Catherine Twomey Fosnot. Portsmouth, NH: Heinemann.

———. 2005c. *Working with the Array, Grades 3–5: Mathematical Models.* CD-ROM with accompanying facilitator's guide by Sherrin B. Hersch, Catherine Twomey Fosnot, and Antonia Cameron. Portsmouth, NH: Heinemann.

Fosnot, Catherine Twomey, and Maarten Dolk. 2002. *Young Mathematicians at Work: Constructing Multiplication and Division.* Portsmouth, NH: Heinemann.

Gravemeijer, Koeno P. E. 1999. How emergent models may foster the constitution of formal mathematics. *Mathematical Thinking and Learning* 1 (2): 155–77.

Karlin, Samuel. 1983. Eleventh R. A. Fisher Memorial Lecture, Royal Society 20.

MULTIPLICATION/DIVISION

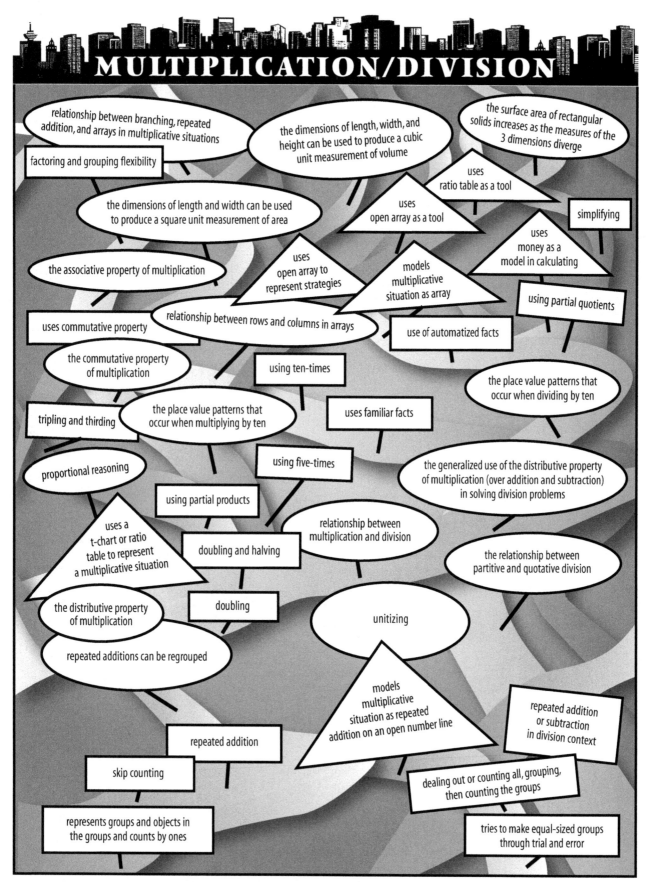

The landscape of learning: multiplication and division on the horizon showing landmark strategies (rectangles), big ideas (ovals), and models (triangles).

Exploring Box Designs

The context of the box factory is introduced to support the development of several big ideas and strategies related to multiplication. Students explore boxes that can each hold 24 items in varying layers. In pairs or groups of three, students work to determine all possible boxes (rectangular prisms) that could hold 24 items arranged in rows, columns, and layers. They also consider the question, how do they know they have identified all the possibilities? A brief math congress is held at the end of the workshop to share helpful strategies and insights gleaned thus far. The investigation will continue on Day Two and a full math congress will not be held until Day Three.

Day One Outline

Developing the Context

☀ Introduce the box context and ask students to investigate all the possible designs of boxes containing 24 items arranged in rows, columns, and layers (three-dimensional arrays).

☀ Explain that acceptable boxes must be rectangular prisms and establish that a box rotated 90 degrees on the same plane (not flipped) is really the same box and thus won't count as another possible design.

☀ Have students use connecting cubes to represent the items in a box.

Supporting the Investigation

☀ Note students' strategies as they explore box designs and encourage them to think about ways to keep track and work more systematically.

Preparing for the Math Congress

☀ Plan a congress discussion that will highlight a few helpful strategies that students can consider as they continue the box investigation on Day Two.

Facilitating the Math Congress

☀ As students discuss their work, record their strategies on chart paper so they can refer back to them on Day Two.

Materials Needed

Box of oranges poster [If you do not have the full-color poster (available from Heinemann), you can use the smaller black-and-white version in Appendix A.]

Connecting cubes—one bin per group of two or three students

Large chart pad and easel (or chalkboard or whiteboard)

Markers

Developing the Context

- ☀ Introduce the box context and ask students to investigate all the possible designs of boxes containing 24 items arranged in rows, columns, and layers (three-dimensional arrays).

- ☀ Explain that acceptable boxes must be rectangular prisms and establish that a box rotated 90 degrees on the same plane (not flipped) is really the same box and thus won't count as another possible design.

- ☀ Have students use connecting cubes to represent the box items.

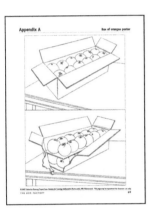

Display the box poster (or Appendix A), showing just the top layer of the box, as you tell the following story:

> *A friend sent me a box of oranges the other day. I opened it up and noticed that the oranges in the box formed an array. See . . . rows and columns. What numbers describe the array of this box?*

When students name the array, write on the chalkboard:

$$2 \times 6 \text{ (held horizontally) or } 6 \times 2 \text{ (held vertically)}$$

Now display the bottom part of the box poster, showing the bottom and top layer of the box, as you continue:

> *Then I discovered that there was another layer of oranges underneath. What is the array for this bottom layer of my box? How many layers are there altogether? How many oranges are there altogether?*

Establish that the box holds 24 oranges, and then write $(2 \times 6) \times 2$, explaining that you are putting the parentheses around the 2×6 because that was the part they calculated first (the amount in the first layer). The "x 2" on the right of the expression represents the two layers. Then continue with the story.

> *This box has a layer on top arranged as a 2 x 6 array and another one just like it on the bottom: 12 oranges in each layer, 2 layers, and 24 oranges in the box.*
>
> *But then I began thinking about boxes in general—not just my box of oranges—and how they come in all different shapes and sizes. Some boxes have only one layer; others have arrangements like a 2 x 2 with many layers, so the boxes are tall. If a box held 24 items and each layer had 2 rows and 2 columns, how many layers would there be?*

Invite discussion, and establish that there would be 6 layers. Acknowledge that although this arrangement might not be ideal for oranges, it is a possible arrangement for 24 items in rows and columns and layers. Write $(2 \times 2) \times 6$ and explain again that you are recording this box arrangement this way since there are 2×2 items in a layer, and there are 6 layers. Then continue:

> *I started to wonder about all the possible arrangements, about box factories where boxes are made, and about how so many things come packaged like this, in rows and columns and layers.*

Before you go on with the story, invite students to recall boxes that they have seen that hold items in three-dimensional arrays: in rows, columns, and layers. Limit the discussion to boxes that are rectangular prisms with three-dimensional arrays of rows, columns, and layers. Some possibilities they might offer are boxes of eggs, chocolates, golf balls, ornaments, glasses, or cups. Then continue:

> *Box factories must have designers—people who decide the size and shape of boxes. What other arrangements do you think there are for 24 items—arrangements of rows and columns with layers? How many possible designs are there?*

Explain that one of the things mathematicians do before they explore a problem is decide how to define it. They decide what will count as a solution or possibility and what won't. They set the parameters. Explain that acceptable boxes must be rectangular prisms and suggest that everyone use parentheses around the arrangement of the layer (as you did) so everyone will know how that box is to be held. Establish that a box rotated 90 degrees on the same plane (not flipped) is really the same box and thus won't count as another possibility: $(4 \times 3) \times 2$ is the same box as $(3 \times 4) \times 2$—a box with two layers of 3×4; it has only been rotated 90 degrees. On the other hand, $(4 \times 2) \times 3$ is a different box. It has been flipped; the bottom is now different and there are three layers of 4×2. Suggest that since connecting cubes might be helpful for this investigation, everyone should explore the problem using a common measurement unit—a connecting cube to represent one item. Facilitate an initial discussion in the meeting area before the students set off to work and establish at least one more possibility to clarify the problem if necessary, such as a box that is $(1 \times 4) \times 6$. Allow students to put forth some thoughts and then suggest that they work as box designers, in pairs or groups of three, to determine all the possible boxes for 24 items made from 24 connecting cubes, arranged in rows, columns, and layers. Have them think about the following questions:

- How many different boxes are there and what are the dimensions?

- How do you know that you have all the possibilities?

Supporting the Investigation

Students should work on this investigation in pairs or in groups of three. Verbal and written communication about their own mathematical thinking is a crucial part of the learning process. It is through listening to and articulating each other's thinking that learners refine their own understanding of the problem and the strategies they are using.

Assign math partners or groups and display the box of oranges poster or Appendix A so all students can see it. Also, connecting cubes should be available. As students work, walk around and take note of the strategies you see. Confer with students as needed to support or challenge their investigation.

Some students may struggle to keep the 24 cubes constant as they manipulate the arrangements and build rectangular prisms with them. Some may fail to include arrangements with more than one layer. Others may struggle to identify boxes that are the same, but just turned—for example, $(3 \times 4) \times 2$ and $(4 \times 3) \times 2$. Per definition, these are the same box. As

☀ Note students' strategies as they explore box designs and encourage them to think about ways to keep track and work more systematically.

students try to find the different possible configurations of boxes holding 24 items, here are a few strategies you might encounter:

✦ Trial and error: building boxes with the cubes and counting the cubes to check whether there are 24

✦ Trial and adjustment: beginning with trial and error, but realizing along the way that the factors of 24 can be helpful, but not using them yet in a systematic fashion

✦ Doubling and halving: starting with a factor pair for 24 and doubling one factor, halving the other [See Figure 1]

✦ Using the associative and commutative properties (although perhaps not explicitly): flipping, for example, a (2 × 6) × 2 box to get a (2 × 2) × 6 box [See Figure 2]

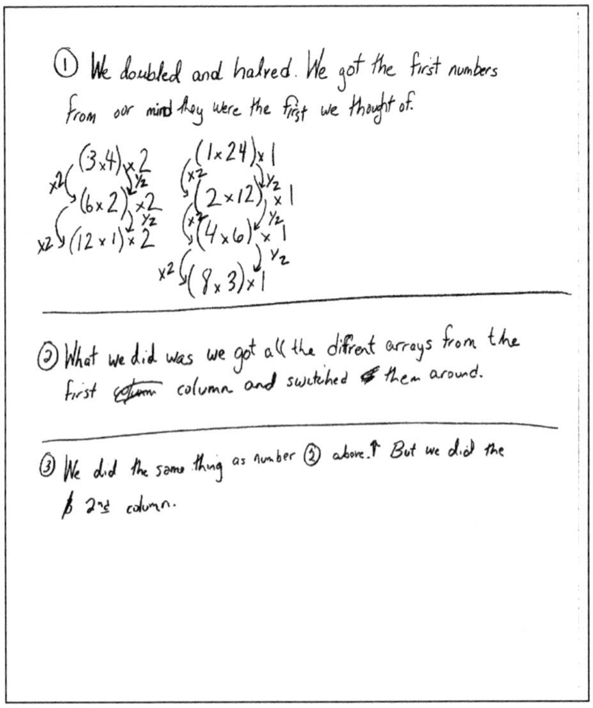

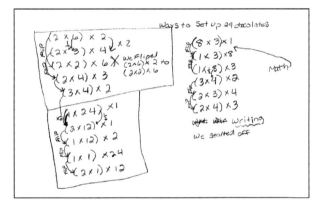

Figure 1

Figure 2

Conferring with Students at Work

Author's Notes

Michelle: How much is that box? *(Pointing to the box being built by her partner, Lori.)*

Lori: It's . . . Here it is. It's 2 by 6 with 2 *(meaning 2 layers.)* OK, um, let's make a 4 by 3.

Miki (the teacher)**:** What do you mean by 4 by 3?

Lori: A 4 by 3 box with 2 of them. *(Showing the two layers by putting one hand over the other.)*

Miki: Oh, OK. So how did you get a 4 by 3 array with 2 layers?

Many students seemingly begin by generating boxes at random. By asking students to share their thinking, Miki encourages them to verbalize and make explicit the specific strategy they are using.

continued on next page

continued from previous page

Lori: I moved this part around. *(Shows a 2 × 3 being taken off the 2 × 6 and moved to make a 4 × 3).*

Miki: Oh, that's an interesting way to find other boxes. Did you see what she did, Michelle?

Michelle: Yeah . . . that's neat. Which is the bottom of your box, though? I'm confused.

Miki: Let's mark the bottom array with parentheses. *(Writes on paper (4 × 3) × 2.)* I'm just going to put parentheses around the 4 × 3 so we know that this is the bottom layer and the 2 means number of layers. Remember? Does that make sense?

Michelle: OK. See here? *(Points to recording sheet.)* We just doubled and halved, um, the 2 × 6. Like the 2 becomes 4 and the 6 is 3. *(Writes on recording sheet (4 × 3) × 2.)*

Miki: I wonder if this doubling and halving strategy will help you find more boxes for 24 items.

It may be challenging for some students to find the words to clarify their thinking—rows, columns, arrays, layers, dimensions. Miki reinforces the vocabulary when conferring with the partnerships. She does this naturally within the context of the conversation.

Michelle and Lori continued to use connecting cubes to build and find more boxes. However, by asking the students to articulate the doubling and halving strategy and to use the parentheses, Miki has helped them to consider a more systematic approach and to keep track of what they have done.

Often the best way to invite an inquiry is to wonder aloud about it. Will doubling and halving produce more possibilities? Miki's question invites a focus on the specific strategy.

Preparing for the Math Congress

After a sufficient amount of time has been devoted to the investigation, ask students to prepare for a brief math congress to discuss strategies they found helpful. It is not expected that students will have completed the investigation today or that they will have worked systematically to derive all the possibilities. They will have time to continue their work on Day Two and they will be supported over the next couple of days in developing a systematic approach to the problem. Have students put their work in their work folders; they do not need to bring it to the congress. Ask them to be prepared to offer one or two helpful insights they had as they worked today.

☀ Plan a congress discussion that will highlight a few helpful strategies that students can consider as they continue the box investigation on Day Two.

Tips for Structuring the Math Congress

It is helpful to think of this first congress as a discussion that will provide support and direction as the work continues on Day Two. Look for students who noticed that flipping a box was helpful in finding another, or for students who doubled and halved. A third possibility is students who are considering how factors might be related, and who could bring the topic up as an insight (rather than as an answer).

Facilitating the Math Congress

☀ As students discuss their work, record their strategies on chart paper so they can refer back to them on Day Two.

Begin by having one or two groups of students share helpful strategies or insights they gleaned as they worked. Do not discuss all the possibilities today. On Day Two, students will work further on this investigation and a full math congress on this investigation will not be held until Day Three. As students share a few helpful strategies or insights, write them down on large chart paper. On Day Two you can display the chart as a helpful reminder before the class returns to work.

A Portion of the Math Congress

Inside One Classroom

Miki (the teacher): So when I walked around today and conferred, I noticed several of you building boxes and then slicing pieces off and attaching them elsewhere to make another box. Michelle and Lori, I saw you doing that. Would you explain to the rest of the class what you were doing?

Lori: We noticed that we could move the cubes around, like doubling and halving.

Miki: Let's build one of the boxes, so you can show us what got halved and what got doubled. *(Miki builds a box, (2 × 6) × 2 with 24 cubes.)* This is the one you had, I think, right?

Lori: Yeah. But we didn't have it all together yet. We just had a 2 by 6 layer and we knew we needed two of them. We cut this part off *(indicates the 2 x 3)* and we moved it over to make a 4 by 3. We still needed 2 layers but it was a different box.

Aaron: Michael and I did something like that, too. We had a 2 by 3 by 4 box. And we sliced the box in half, sort of. See? Now it's a 2 by 3 by 2. We moved the other half down and attached it here and now it is a 2 by 6 by 2.

Miki: Interesting. How many of you used a strategy sort of like this . . . doubling and halving? *(Four or five hands go up.)* We'll be working on this investigation again tomorrow so for now let's post some of these helpful ideas we are sharing. *(Writes "doubling and halving" on the chart paper.)* Any other helpful ideas? Sherrie?

continued on next page

Author's Notes

Miki encourages the students to do the explaining. The ideas are theirs and they are being asked to share with their fellow mathematicians. Subtly Miki is developing a sense of community.

The students are expected to comment on each other's ideas and to see how they are similar to their own. Miki encourages dialogue to flow from student to student.

continued from previous page

Sherrie: I think factors have something to do with it.

Miki: Tell us more. What do you mean?

Sherrie: I don't know. But all the numbers we found that worked so far are factors of 24, like 2 and 6, and 3 and 4.

Miki: That's interesting, isn't it? Let's get that on our chart. Tomorrow we can think about that further, too.

The ideas are simply recorded on the chart for now rather than being discussed thoroughly. On Day Two students will have a chance to return to work and try them out.

Reflections on the Day

Observing students at work today allowed you to see the variety of big ideas and strategies they are constructing about multiplication. Their work today was most likely not systematic, although in the math congress they had a chance to begin consideration of some helpful strategies. On Day Two they will return to work on this investigation, and try out the strategies offered in discussion.

Exploring Box Designs

Materials Needed

Graph paper arrays, cut to match the problems in the minilesson (see page 21), and scissors

Box of oranges poster (or Appendix A)

Students' work from Day One

Chart of strategies from Day One

Connecting cubes—one bin per group of two or three students

Drawing paper—a few sheets per group of two or three students

Large chart paper—one sheet per group of two or three students

Large chart pad and easel

Markers

Today begins with a minilesson on doubling and halving. This is a strategy that students may use to find all possible designs for boxes holding 24 items. Students will then continue to work with their math partners to investigate and refine their thinking about this problem, and about how they know that they have found all the possible box configurations for 24 items. They will also prepare for Day Three's math congress by creating posters that show their thinking. Developing posters allows students to reflect on their work, and may challenge them to generalize their thinking.

Day Two Outline

Minilesson: A Multiplication String

☀ Work on a string of problems designed to encourage the use of doubling and halving.

☀ Use graph paper arrays to represent students' strategies.

Supporting the Investigation

☀ Re-examine the chart of strategies from Day One and ask students to resume their investigations.

☀ As students work, encourage them to consider ways to keep track of all the possible arrangements and challenge them to justify that they have found them all.

Preparing for the Math Congress

☀ Ask students to prepare posters of their work that reflect not only the possible arrangements they found, but also their justifications for knowing they've found them all.

☀ Plan to focus the congress on the associative and commutative properties and scaffold the discussion to highlight the value of working systematically.

Minilesson: A Multiplication String (10–15 minutes)

This mental math minilesson uses a string of related problems designed to encourage students to use multiplication facts they already know to figure out other, more difficult ones. It is assumed that students working on this unit may not have automatized the multiplication facts yet, and the strings in this unit are designed to help them do so by focusing on relationships. The string also supports doubling and halving. Do one problem at a time, allowing think time before you start discussion. Use graph paper arrays and have scissors handy to cut them to match students' strategies. For example, if a student says, "I cut a 6 by 8 in half to make a 12 by 4," cut a 6×8 array into two 6×4 arrays and then place one above the other to make a new 2-D array, 12×4. Invite students to discuss the connection with the work they did on Day One.

☀ Work on a string of problems designed to encourage the use of doubling and halving.

☀ Use graph paper arrays to represent students' strategies.

String of related problems:

3×4

3×8

6×8

12×4

24×2

48×1

3×16

Behind the Numbers

The first three problems are basic facts but they are presented one at a time and related in a way that supports the use of doubling (each one is double the previous one). The next three problems in the string are all equivalent because one factor doubles while the other halves. Even if students do not use doubling and halving to produce the answers, the fact that the answers are the same will likely engender a discussion on equivalence. The doubling and halving are not as easy to see in the last problem; students must look back over the string. And now, since the answer is the same as in the previous problems, new relationships can be examined.

A Portion of the Minilesson

Inside One Classroom

Miki (the teacher): *(Writes on the chalkboard 6 × 8.)* Here is the next one . . . another multiplication fact. What is 6 times 8? Chas?

Chas: That's 48.

Miki: *(Writes 48 next to the problem and puts a 6 × 8 array up next to the problem.)* Great, and here's a 6 by 8 array I cut out. Can somebody show us how this is a 6 by 8 array? Megan?

Megan: There's 6 squares going down and 8 going across. *(Points to the columns and rows of the array.)*

continued on next page

Author's Notes

Automatizing the basic multiplication facts is critical when moving on to more challenging multiplication problems.

The purpose of using the array is to provide students with a representation of their strategies. Eventually the array will become a tool with which to think.

continued from previous page

Miki: So 6 squares in the column and each one is in a row. Everybody agrees that we have 6 rows and 8 columns? *(Nods from the class.)* OK, here's another problem. *(Writes 12 × 4 directly underneath the first problem.)* Take a minute to think about how you would solve this problem. When you are ready, put a thumb up so you don't disturb other people who are still working on it. *(Waits a few seconds before calling on students to share.)* Debbie?

Although Megan is describing the number of squares in the column, these squares also designate the number of rows. Miki rephrases. Coordinating rows and columns can be quite difficult for students.

Debbie: Well, I just knew it. I knew 12 × 4 was 48. But I also noticed that it's the same answer as 6 × 8.

Miki: That's interesting, Debbie. Did anybody else notice that? I wonder why that happened.

One of the reasons that each problem in a string is written directly below the previous one is that observations such as Debbie's can be made more easily.

Claire: I think you double and halve 6 × 8 so it's the same answer.

Miki: Can you say more about that, Claire?

Miki asks Claire to expand on her thinking in order to encourage conversation on this important strategy.

Claire: Well, 12 is double 6 and 4 is half of 8 so the answer is still 48.

Miki: *(Draws an arrow from the 6 to the 12 and from the 8 to the 4 and writes × 2 and × ¹/₂, respectively, next to the arrows.)* Claire, can you show us how the doubling and halving works using the 6 × 8 array?

Claire: You cut the 6 by 8 array in half. So you count 4 squares across and cut down the line there. *(Uses scissors to cut the 6 × 8 array in half vertically.)* And then you take one of the pieces and connect it to the bottom of the other piece so you have 12 squares going down. *(Attaches one 6 × 4 piece to the bottom of the other 6 × 4 piece to make a 12 × 4.)* That's a 12 by 4 array now, and you still have 48.

The paper array is cut and moved to represent Claire's thinking.

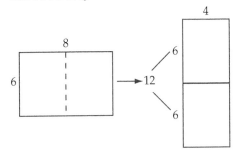

Miki: This is interesting. Let's think about the next problem, and how the array can be doubled and halved like Claire just did. Here it is: 24 × 2. *(Writes 24 × 2 directly under 12 × 4.)*

Supporting the Investigation

☀ Re-examine the chart of strategies from Day One and ask students to resume their investigations.

☀ As students work, encourage them to consider ways to keep track of all the possible arrangements and challenge them to justify that they have found them all.

After the minilesson, display the box of oranges poster (or Appendix A) and remind students about the investigation they began on Day One and re-examine the chart that describes their helpful strategies. If doubling and halving is not on your chart, ask students if they think this might be a helpful strategy, and then add it to the chart. Distribute connecting cubes and drawing paper and ask students to resume their work from Day One. Remind them that the purpose is to find all the boxes and to be certain that they have all possibilities.

Today you will probably see more systematic approaches than you did on Day One. A few students may still be using trial and error, but many will use doubling and halving. Some will systematically start with one-layer boxes, generating all possible arrays, and then explore two-layer boxes and so on. As you move around the room conferring with students, suggest that if they want to be sure they have all of the possible boxes, they might want to think of a way to keep track. As the investigation continues, some students will still need time to think about helpful strategies, explore them, and own them. You can challenge students to think about how they know for certain that they have all the different boxes that can hold 24 items. It is one thing to say they have all the boxes, and quite another to justify such a claim. To meet this challenge, students will now have to think about how to organize their solutions and determine whether some of their solutions are duplicates. They will also have to think about what might serve as a justification. This is a huge step for students on the landscape of learning, but a necessary one in the development of their mathematical thinking.

Conferring with Students at Work

Inside One Classroom

Author's Notes

David: *(Holds a (2 × 6) × 2 box made of cubes in his hand and flips it around.)* I have another one. It's a 2 by 2 by 6 box.

Chloe: *(Mumbles quietly, not sure if what she is saying is accurate.)* That's the same.

Miki (the teacher): *(Hears Chloe's comment and encourages the partners to discuss her observation.)* Wait a second. Sound the alarm! I heard Chloe say something interesting. Can you share your thinking with David?

Chloe: I think that's the same box.

David: *(still holding the original box.)* Well, it is the same and it's different. It's like what Zach said. These two boxes *(shows the 2 × 6 × 2, then flips it to show 2 × 2 × 6)* are congruent. But they're different because one has only 2 layers and this one has 6.

Chloe: I think they're still the same. David just flipped it to make the one with 6 layers.

Miki: So the dimensions are the same but the box has been flipped to make a new box. Now the bottom is different and the number of layers is different. You just flipped the 2 by 6 by 2 to get 2 by 2 by 6. How can we write that?

David: We can just write it like this and say that we flipped it. *(Writes the two problems one underneath the other and draws an arrow connecting the two problems with the word* flipped *written next to it.)*

Miki: Great. Do you think we can do that with these other boxes you found? How about this one, 3 by 8 by 1?

This discussion facilitated by Miki is critical in developing the students' understanding of the associative and commutative properties of multiplication.

One of the challenging things about observing and conferring with students is being able to identify those moments when we ask students to dig deeper and pursue a certain line of inquiry that may lead to a big understanding.

Miki supports David and Chloe by encouraging them to begin thinking about the problem in a systematic way. How can they begin organizing their information so they can work more efficiently and eliminate duplicates?

Preparing for the Math Congress

☀ Ask students to prepare posters of their work that reflect not only the possible arrangements they found, but also their justifications for knowing they've found them all.

☀ Plan to focus the congress on the associative and commutative properties and scaffold the discussion to highlight the value of working systematically.

As students finish up their work, ask them to make posters that depict the important things they will want to share in the math congress on Day Three. When mathematicians write up their findings for math journals, they do not merely reiterate everything they did. Instead, they focus on crafting a convincing and elegant argument or proof for other mathematicians to consider. This communication is an important part of mathematics. Of course, elementary students will not be expected to write formal proofs, but by focusing on the justification and logic of their arguments regarding how they know for certain they have found all the possibilities, you are helping them develop the ability to write up their ideas for presentation to a mathematical community. Encourage students to make posters that not only show the possibilities they found, but also demonstrate how they know for certain they have found all of them. On Day Three you will be holding a math congress on this work.

▦ Tips for Structuring the Math Congress

Using your notes, think about a structure for the math congress that will support students in their understanding of the big ideas and strategies related to multiplication. Consider how you can scaffold strategy development toward the value of working systematically and focus a discussion on the associative and commutative properties of multiplication. To accomplish these goals, some teachers have found it helpful to select pieces of work that illustrate the following:

✦ Flipping and turning to produce other boxes even though the work is not systematic and some boxes are the same. This gives you a chance to discuss the associative property—flipping, $(2 \times 3) \times 4 = 2 \times (3 \times 4)$—and the commutative property—turning, $(2 \times 3) \times 4 = (3 \times 2) \times 4$. [See Figure 3]

✦ A more systematic approach—for example, using doubling and halving consistently, even if some of the boxes found are duplicates or a few are missing. This gives you a chance to suggest that students think of ways to keep track to ensure that duplicates aren't listed and all possibilities have been found. Note: If students have doubled and halved, they may have missed $(1 \times 3) \times 8$ and $(3 \times 4) \times 2$. [See Figure 4]

2X16X1

# sentence	column	Row	Layers	
2x12x1	2	+6 12	1	✓
(1X24)x1	1	24	1	✓
(3X8)X1	3	8	1	✓
(4x6)x1	4	6	1	✓
(4x3)x2	4	3	2	✓
(2x4)x3	2	4	3	
(1x6)x4	1	6	4	
(1x12)x2	1	12	2	
(6x2)x2	6	2	2	
(2x2)x6	2	2	6	
(1x1)x24	1	1	24	✓
(2x3)x4	2	3	4	
(1x8)x3	1	8	3	
(3x1)x8	3	1	8	
(4x1)x6	4	1	6	

Figure 3

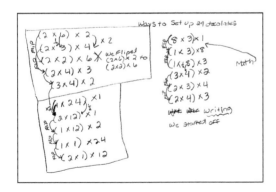

Figure 4

✦ Keeping the layers consistent and systematically finding all possibilities for one layer, then two, then three, etc. This gives you a chance to examine all the factors of 24 and a systematic way to use them to determine all of the 16 possible combinations of factors. [See Figure 5]

Sequencing your congress toward valuing systematic work, as above, may support students' progressive development by providing scaffolding.

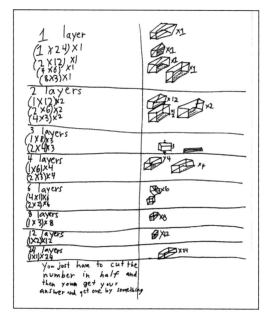

Figure 5

Reflections on the Day

Today students were encouraged to develop a systematic approach to solving the problem of designing boxes. In developing their posters, they had to think about how to organize their information so that their work over the last two days could be conveyed to the whole group in a clear, concise, and thoughtful way.

Exploring Box Designs

Materials Needed

Students' posters from Day Two

Before class, display these around the meeting area.

Sticky notes—one pad per student

Connecting cubes—one bin per group of two or three students

Today begins with a "gallery walk," during which students look at each other's posters and record comments to share with the authors. This is an opportunity for your students to re-familiarize themselves in the context and mathematics of the problem considered on Days One and Two. After the walk, you will facilitate a math congress—a whole-group discussion of the strategies students used on Days One and Two as they investigated the different box designs for 24 items, and of how they know that they found all the possibilities. The congress gives you a chance to focus on the students' work, and to discuss systematic approaches and the application of the associative and commutative properties of multiplication.

Day Three Outline

Preparing for the Math Congress (continued from Day Two)

☀ Conduct a gallery walk to give students a chance to review and comment on each other's posters.

Facilitating the Math Congress

☀ Facilitate a discussion of the posters you have chosen and be sure that students discuss how they know they have found all the possible arrangements.

Preparing for the Math Congress (continued from Day Two)

Explain that before students start the math congress, they will have a gallery walk to look at each other's posters. Pass out small pads of sticky notes and suggest that students use them to record comments or questions, and then place them directly on the posters. Give students about fifteen minutes to read and comment on the mathematics on the posters. Then give everyone a few minutes to read the comments and questions on their own posters. The gallery walk allows your students to revisit and reflect on the problem, and to comment on each other's mathematical thinking and the representation of that thinking.

You may need to model for your students how to comment in helpful, appropriate ways. You might write, "I think your strategy is interesting, and I'm trying to figure out why we don't have the same number of boxes." Or "You explained your work really well. I can understand what you did and I am convinced you have found them all." Or "It's hard for me to follow your thinking. How do you know you have them all?" Or "Your poster really convinces me. I agree with your thinking." Or "Your strategy is really great. What made you think of starting like that?" Or "Your way is so fast. I want to try that strategy next time!" Or "I'm puzzled about this box. Isn't that the same box as this one, just turned around? I need more convincing."

☀ Conduct a gallery walk to give students a chance to review and comment on each other's posters.

Facilitating the Math Congress

Once the gallery walk has been completed, convene students in the meeting area to discuss the pieces of work you have chosen to highlight in the math congress. In the order that you've chosen, ask students to explain the strategies they used. As appropriate, encourage students to make connections among their classmates' posters.

☀ Facilitate a discussion of the posters you have chosen and be sure that students discuss how they know they have found all the possible arrangements.

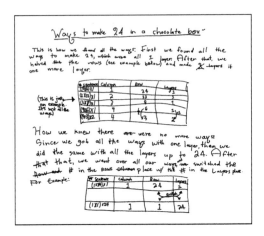

Author's Notes

Tim: First we started with all the one-layer boxes. *(Points to the chart on their poster that shows boxes with one layer.)* Then we halved this row *(points to the (4 × 6) × 1 box)* and doubled the number of layers and got 4 by 3 by 2.

Mary: How we knew that there were no more ways [to make boxes for 24 items] was because we started with all the ways for one layer, and then we found all the different ones for each layer up to 24. So we switched the number in the rows with the number in the layers, and this is our example. We had (1 × 24) × 1, and we made it (1 × 1) × 24 because we switched this number here with this number there. *(Points to the poster to indicate the numbers being switched.)*

Chas: That was kind of another strategy. We did that with all the other boxes, and after we made sure we didn't do double the same boxes.

(The three students pause and wait for questions from the class. Chas calls on Chloe, who has raised her hand.)

Chloe: Right down there, I don't exactly get what you did. *(Points to the bottom of the poster, which explains how the group "switched numbers.")*

Chas: Well, here *(points to the written explanation on the poster)* we wrote that since we have all the ways for one layer, we did the same thing for all the layers up to 24. So we switched the numbers in the rows place with the numbers in the layers to get all the ways. We had the columns stay the same, but these 2 *(points to the rows and layers)* were reversed and it's a different box.

(Chloe continues to look confused.)

Miki (the teacher): Mary, Chas, and Tim, I think what some people might be confused about is what you mean by "switched the numbers." When you're switching numbers around, what exactly is happening with the box? If you can show us using the box, it might make it clearer for some people who are still confused.

continued on next page

Mary, Chas, and Tim's poster is displayed on the chalkboard so they and the class can refer to it as the group shares. Mary, Chas, and Tim are at the front sharing their work. Miki is sitting among the students.

This portion of the congress focuses on the question of how the students know that they have all the possibilities. By digging deeper into this question and having this particular group share their strategy and understanding, Miki supports the development of understanding of the associative and commutative properties of multiplication.

Miki notices that as the group is sharing, the language they are using ("ways, switching numbers, reversed") to explain their work is straying from the original context of the problem. In order to clarify the switching-numbers strategy, Miki refocuses the discussion around the original context, the boxes. Staying within the context provides students with a concrete tool with which to mathematize the situation.

continued from previous page

Chas: OK, well, this is 2 by 6 by 2. *(Holding a (2 × 6) × 2 box made of cubes.)* So it's 2, 6, 2. *(Points to the chart on the poster, where 2 is in the column labeled "column," 6 is in the column labeled "row," and 2 is in the column labeled "layer.")* So this is the box flat. And then we changed it and made it tall. *(Takes the same box and flips it so it is now a box with 6 layers).* So now it has 6 layers and each layer is 2 by 2. So the 6 and the 2 were switched. Like a 1 by 24 by 1 is long *(stretches out his arms to the left and right to demonstrate)*, but if we change it this way *(stretches out his arms vertically)* it becomes really tall. Then it's 1 by 1 on the bottom with a lot of layers, 24.

Development of a strong learning community is critical to facilitating a math congress in which students feel safe sharing, taking risks, and asking questions when confused.

Miki: How many of you found that you could turn and flip? Sometimes just turning got you the same box, didn't it? But flipping gave you a different box bottom. For example, here's one . . . *(writes (2 × 3) × 4)* If 2 by 3 is the bottom and you have 4 layers, you can move the parentheses to get a new bottom and get 2 by 3 by 4. Actually the box flipped. It's still 24 items but now we have 2 layers and each layer is 3 by 4.

Katie: It's like you still have the same factors but you're grouping them differently.

Miki: Isn't that interesting about multiplication? We can group the factors in different ways but we still get the same answer!

Miki encourages the generalization of the associative property.

Assessment Tips

The posters are probably too large to place in students' portfolios. If so, take a photograph of each one and staple it to a blank page for your anecdotal notes. Make notes about the strategies and big ideas described on the landscape of learning graphic (page 11). Do you have evidence that any of these ideas and strategies have been constructed?

Over the course of the unit, you might want to keep all student work together. This work can be examined with students on Day Ten as a way to reflect on their learning of the past two weeks. This work can then be used to create a learning wall for reflection.

Reflections on the Day

Today's math congress was a critical steppingstone in the development of several big ideas related to multiplication. The work that each group shared was chosen specifically to evoke systematic approaches, and the big ideas of the commutative and associative properties. Students were encouraged to look at each other's work, make comments, ask questions, and learn from each other. They were able to monitor their own understanding about the work that was shared during the math congress. The ideas and strategies discussed will be further developed as the unit progresses.

DAY FOUR

How Much Cardboard Is Needed?

Materials Needed

Graph paper arrays, cut to match the problems in the minilesson (see page 31), and scissors

Students' posters from Day Two

Student recording sheet for the cardboard investigation (Appendix B)—one per group of two to four students

Connecting cubes—one bin per group of two to four students

Scissors—one pair per group of two to four students

Drawing paper or graph paper (with squares that match the size of connecting cubes you have been using)—a few sheets per group of two to four students

Large chart pad and easel

Markers

Today begins with a minilesson on the use of partial products: specifically on the use of ten-times and place value patterns. Underlying this strategy is the use of the distributive and associative properties of multiplication. Students will then build on the work of the first investigation by exploring the cheapest and the most expensive cardboard boxes possible for 24 items—learning that the closer the box is to a cube, the less cardboard is needed. The cardboard box problem allows students to deepen their understanding of the associative property, and supports their evolving understanding of surface area and its relationship to volume.

Day Four Outline

Minilesson: A Multiplication String

* Work on a string of problems designed to encourage using ten-times and using partial products.
* Use graph paper arrays to represent students' strategies.

Developing the Context

* Introduce a new context involving an exploration of the amount of cardboard needed to manufacture boxes and whether some box designs would be cheaper to manufacture than others.

Supporting the Investigation

* Ask students to cut out arrays to represent the surface areas of the boxes.
* Encourage students to consider the relationship between surface area and volume.

Minilesson: A Multiplication String (10–15 minutes)

Today's mental math string, similar to the string from Day Two, encourages students to use multiplication facts that they know to figure out more difficult problems. This particular string supports the associative property of multiplication and the use of ten-times. Toward the end of the string students are challenged to make partial products (using the distributive property). Again, do one problem at a time, giving enough think time before you start the discussion. Use the precut graph paper arrays to represent students' strategies. Invite students to discuss the relationship between the problems in the string. If students perform the standard paper/pencil multiplication algorithm to solve 4×39, encourage them to think about what is happening. For example, when students say, "Then I multiplied 4 by the 3" (from the 30), ask them to find where the 3 is on the graph paper array. See if they realize that the 3 refers to 3 tens, or 30. Invite students to make connections between the standard algorithm and other strategies that have been shared. The standard multiplication algorithm is based on the distributive property, as with the strategies described in Behind the Numbers.

- ☀ Work on a string of problems designed to encourage using ten-times and using partial products.

- ☀ Use graph paper arrays to represent students' strategies.

Behind the Numbers

The first and third problems in the string are basic facts that are related to the second and fourth problems, respectively. Each coupling supports the development of the associative property. For example, 2×30 can be thought of as $2 \times (3 \times 10)$ or $(2 \times 3) \times 10$. The last two problems in the string support students' move toward making use of the distributive property of multiplication to aid in computation. The 4×41 is just one more group of four. For the last problem, some students might split 39 and calculate $(4 \times 30) + (4 \times 9)$ and add the partial products together, $120 + 36 = 156$. Other students might notice a connection to the previous two problems. For example, $4 \times 39 = 4 \times (40 - 1) = (4 \times 40) - (4 \times 1)$.

String of related problems:

$$2 \times 3$$
$$2 \times 30$$
$$4 \times 4$$
$$4 \times 40$$
$$4 \times 41$$
$$4 \times 39$$

A Portion of the Minilesson

Inside One Classroom

Author's Notes

Miki (the teacher): Here's 2×3, which Lori just said was 6. And here is the array for 2×3. *(Displays a precut graph paper array of 2×3 next to the problem.)* I'm going to write another problem on the board. Before you raise your hand, I want you to take a look at it and think about what the array for this new problem might look like. *(Writes 2×30 directly underneath the first problem in the string. Pauses to give students think time.)* Megan?

Megan: It's 60. And I think the array is going to be long and short. *(Gestures with her hands.)*

Notice that Miki does not ask for the answer to the problem 2 x 30 right away. Instead, she focuses the discussion on the array.

continued on next page

continued from previous page

Miki: *(Displays a precut array of 2 × 30 next to the problem.)* Megan, how did you get 60? Can you talk about that?

Megan: Well, I knew that 30 + 30 equals 60. But another way is that I know that 2 × 3 is 6, and if you add a zero to the 3, then you just add a zero to the 6.

Miki: Hmmm, but usually when I add zero to a number, my answer is the same. For example, if I add a zero to the 3 here, like you said, 3 + 0 is 3. Are we really adding a zero? What's happening here? *(One or two hands go up. Most students stare blankly.)* OK, turn to a neighbor and talk about this question. What is really happening when we put a zero at the end of the number?

(Students turn to each other to discuss this question. Miki listens in on their conversations. The following is an excerpt from one of these conversations.)

Chas: I think there's 10 of the 2 by 3s. I think that's what it means.

Miki: Thomas and Joe, what do you think about what Chas just said? Do you agree? Disagree?

Thomas: I agree with Chas.

Miki: Joe, do you think you can restate what Chas said in your own words? Thomas, do you think it would help if Joe also used the arrays to explain what Chas said?

Thomas: Yeah, I'm a little confused.

Joe: *(Turns to Chas.)* Well, you said that there's 10 of the 2 by 3s. Right? Like if you take the 2 by 3 array, and you count 10 times, it would fit inside the 2 by 30 array.

Miki: Can you show us what you mean by count 10 times? Go ahead and use the arrays on the board.

Joe: See, you do this. *(Lays the 2 × 3 array on top of the 2 × 30, matching up the rows, and then slides the 2 × 3 array across the 2 × 30 array, counting the number of times the 2 × 3 array fits.)* So that's 1, 2, 3, 4, 5, . . . 10.

(Returning to the whole group.)

Miki: I listened in on an interesting conversation that Thomas, Joe, and Chas were having. Chas, can you represent the group and share what you discussed?

Chas: We noticed that there are ten 2 by 3s in 2 by 30. So if you make ten 2 by 3 arrays, it would add up to 60.

continued on next page

The "adding-zero" method is a trick that students often use when multiplying by ten or multiples of ten.

Miki invites students to dig deeper into the workings of this trick in order to understand what is happening mathematically. By asking what is really happening when they "add" a zero, Miki has created confusion among the students. This disequilibrium is a necessary step in the development of an understanding of the mathematics behind the "trick."

Miki provides students with the chance to slow down, reflect on and make sense of something that was previously a rote procedure.

In addition to the math lesson, Miki is also thinking about how she can support her students to become accountable participants during whole- and small-group conversations. She encourages students to ask questions when they are confused and to clarify their thinking, not for her, but for each other. She wants her students to feel responsible to each other, not just to her, the teacher.

Miki does not do the explaining. Students are encouraged to explain to the community.

continued from previous page

Miki: *(Writes (2 × 3) × 10 = 2 × (3 × 10) = 60 on the board.)* Let's try it. I'm going to draw a line every time we have a 2 by 3 array on the 2 by 30 array. Could you count aloud together?

A specific case of the use of the associative property is being examined here.

Class: One, 2, 3, 4, 5, . . . 10. (Miki draws a line for every 2 × 3 array inside the 2 × 30 array.)

Students often need to physically check the relationship. Using the array allows them to do so.

Miki: That's interesting. So there are ten 2 by 3 small arrays. But it seems like magic when I add 6 + 6 + 6 + 6—10 of them—and always land on a number with a zero on the end. Why does this happen?

Chloe: I think it's because you also have 6 tens. You can turn it around. 10 × 6 = 6 × 10. So the number goes to the tens place.

The commutative property explains why the digits "bump" over a place: 10 × 6 = 6 × 10.

Developing the Context

Display students' posters from the math congress on Day Two. Build a (1 × 24) × 1 box using the connecting cubes and display for the class to see. Then introduce the new context for the investigation with the following story:

☀ Introduce a new context involving an exploration of the amount of cardboard needed to manufacture boxes and whether some box designs would be cheaper to manufacture than others.

> *We spent the last couple of days investigating all the different boxes for 24 items. We talked about how we knew we had all the possibilities, and we're confident that we've found them all. We found some boxes for 24 items that had pretty interesting dimensions, like the (1 x 24) x 1. Imagine this box and trying to buy it at the store. When I imagined what this box would look like, I began to think about the amount of cardboard needed in the manufacturing of each of the boxes. I started to wonder, would all our designs require the same amount of cardboard? If not: since it costs money to buy cardboard to make the boxes, would some of them be cheaper to manufacture? Would some be more expensive?*

Before students set off to work, facilitate a brief conversation at the meeting area to share initial thoughts and theories and to provide clarity for students who have questions about the new investigation. Some students may ask about the lids of the boxes and argue that they might be different. If needed, use the cube boxes poster (or Appendix D), and point out that the covers you have in mind are really just an array as well with a small tab insert and since all the boxes would have a similar insert the class can ignore those.

Behind the Numbers

The first part of this unit explored various three-dimensional arrays for arranging 24 items in a box, using cubes to represent the items. Using parentheses to differentiate the rows and columns of the layer array from the number of layers, students found all the different ways to arrange 24 items (cubes) in rectangular prisms. To build on this initial investigation, students will now explore the surface area of these boxes and the relationship of surface area to volume. The faces become smaller the closer you get to a cube thereby requiring less cardboard and making a cube the cheapest box to manufacture.

This new exploration is also designed to get students to realize the congruency of some of the boxes and to ensure the development of the associative and commutative properties. For example, students might notice that the cost of cardboard for a (3 × 8) × 1 box will be the same for a (3 × 1) × 8 and a (1 × 8) × 3 box. They may apply this observation to other boxes, making it a generalization.

Supporting the Investigation

* Ask students to cut out arrays to represent the surface areas of the boxes.

* Encourage students to consider the relationship between surface area and volume.

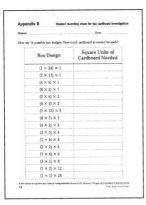

Students can probably work on this problem in groups of four, combining partnerships from previous days. (Note: If you find group dynamics in your class difficult, you might prefer to continue to use pairs.) Distribute recording sheets (Appendix B) and blank paper or graph paper so students can cut out the arrays for the surface areas. Remind students that everyone agreed to use cubes as the unit when they designed the boxes, so they can use the graph paper now, since the squares are the same size as the connecting cubes, to represent the box sides made of cardboard. [Note: The graph paper can be used only if the squares match the size of the connecting cubes used previously. If not, give students blank paper and have them draw outlines of the faces by tracing around the boxes made of cubes and drawing in lines to represent the rows and columns.] Students can then count each square on the paper as a unit to calculate the cost of the boxes. For example, students can calculate the surface area of a box with the dimensions $(1 \times 24) \times 1$ by noting 24 square units on 4 faces and 1 square unit at each end of the box, thereby coming to a total of 98 square units of cardboard.

Students should also have access to their posters from Day Two to remind them of the arrangements they found. If some students did not find all 16 possibilities, you might want to match them with a group that did, although this is not necessary since the recording sheet lists the 16 possible boxes.

More students may need to use the connecting cubes for this part of the investigation since it can be challenging to visualize a three-dimensional figure and mentally manipulate it to picture the arrays that form the faces of each box. Moreover, students may find it difficult to draw a three-dimensional figure on paper. For these reasons, many students may need to actually build the boxes in order to determine the surface area of each box.

Conferring with Students at Work

Inside One Classroom

Author's Notes

In this conversation, David and Sherrie begin to develop a theory about the relationship between surface area and volume.

David: *(Holding a (1 × 24) × 1 box made out of connecting cubes.)* Sherrie, if I cut this in half and make a 1 by 12 by 2 box, it'll be cheaper, I think.

Sherrie: Let's count it.

David: No, no, we don't need to count it. Look, it has less squares showing.

continued on next page

continued from previous page

Miki (the teacher)**:** That's interesting, what you just did there, David. You knew that the 1 by 12 by 2 box would be cheaper than the 1 by 24 by 1 box, but you didn't even count the squares on the outside. Can you explain how you knew it would be cheaper without counting the squares? Sherrie, what do you think? Would it help if David explained it a bit more?

Miki works to ensure that Sherrie understands what David is considering.

Sherrie: I think I know what he's talking about, but I'm not sure.

David: OK, I took the 1 by 24 by 1 box *(returns the connecting cubes to the initial dimensions)* and see how all these squares are showing on the outside? *(Points to the top face of the box.)* If I cut this box in half like this *(breaks the (1 × 24) × 1 box to make two (1 × 12) × 1 boxes)* and attach it here *(reattaches the two new boxes to make one two-layer box (1 × 12) × 2)*, see all the squares that are now covered up? They're inside the box now and you can't see them. So I know there's going to be less cardboard needed, because 24 squares got covered, 12 from this one and 12 from the other one. This new box is cheaper.

Miki: What do you think, Sherrie?

Sherrie: I agree with David, and I think if we keep breaking it in half and making new boxes, there'll be more inside so it'll be cheaper because there's less squares showing.

Miki: That's an interesting theory. Before you go on, do you think you can make a prediction about which of these boxes (points to the recording sheet that lists the different boxes) would be the cheapest and which would be the most expensive?

Asking students to make predictions based on their theories encourages them not only to test their ideas, but also to make generalizations. Miki encourages both students to generalize and reflect on David's idea by asking them to predict.

Reflections on the Day

Today you built on the big ideas explored in the math congress on Day Three, beginning with a minilesson using multiplication strings to further develop understanding of the associative property. Today's follow-up investigation allowed students to revisit the box factory context, but this time to think about the relationship between surface area and volume, to examine how multiplication is related both to the surface area and to the total number of cubic units in the box, and to continue to explore arrays (both two-dimensional and three-dimensional). On Day Five students will finish their work, prepare for a math congress by making posters, and then meet to discuss their conclusions.

DAY FIVE

How Much Cardboard Is Needed?

Materials Needed

Box of oranges poster (or Appendix A)

Students' work from Day Four

Connecting cubes—one bin per group of two to four students

Scissors and tape or glue for each group of two to four students

Drawing paper or graph paper (with squares that match the size of connecting cubes you have been using)—a few sheets per group of two to four students

Large chart paper—one sheet per group of two to four students

Markers

Today students make posters of their work and share their results and conclusions in small groups as preparation for the math congress. This discussion allows students to refine their thinking about this problem. Then a math congress is held to discuss the amount of cardboard needed for each box—and to generalize the relationship between surface area and volume.

Day Five Outline

Preparing for the Math Congress

* Ask students to finish up their investigations and make posters of their work.
* Have students facilitate small-group discussions of their work as a way to help refine their thinking.
* Plan for a congress discussion on the relationship between surface area and volume and on deepening students' understanding of the associative and commutative properties.

Facilitating the Math Congress

* As students share their strategies, encourage the class to generalize the relationship between surface area and volume.

Preparing for the Math Congress

Begin today's math workshop in the meeting area. Display the box of oranges poster (or Appendix A) and remind students about the investigation they began on Day Four. Ask students to resume their work, reminding them that the task is to find the boxes that require the most cardboard to make, and those that require the least. Ask them also to create posters for the math congress so they can convince the community of their findings. The process of writing up the posters pushes students to organize their thinking about the problem. They will need to think about clarity and conciseness in conveying their work to the whole class. It can be a challenge for students at this age to distinguish between essential and nonessential pieces of information in the effort to communicate their work most effectively. Encourage students to glue or tape paper cutouts of the surface area of the boxes onto their posters in order to illustrate their thinking.

Sometimes teachers support students' understanding of the strategies and big ideas in a mathematical investigation by conducting small-group discussions prior to the whole-class congress. This test run allows students to present their work to a smaller audience and get feedback. It also gives students who may not feel comfortable in large group settings more opportunity to participate in the conversation and to take greater risks. Most important, however, these small-group discussions allow students to deepen their thinking about the problem and refine their work.

It is important to note that the students facilitate the small-group discussions. For this reason, it is critical to choose the participants carefully. Think about who would benefit most from conversation in a small group. Consider students' mathematical understanding of the problem and ability to work independently. Students participating in the small-group discussion should be able not only to monitor their own contribution to the discussion, but also to mediate the flow of the conversation. Students should be comfortable enough to maintain accountability among the group members by asking each other questions and exchanging comments such as "You look confused. Do you want me to restate what I just said?" or "I'm still not getting it. Can you talk more about what you just said?" or "I disagree/agree with that because . . ." The small-group discussions should be done after you have provided extensive modeling of accountable talking and sharing and after students have had plenty of experience with the whole-class math congress.

Give students an opportunity to refine their posters in order to take into account the feedback from the small-group discussion. While they are doing so, think about how you will structure the conversation in the congress. Which groups will you ask to share? In what order? Why? How will your choice facilitate development?

- Ask students to finish up their investigations and make posters of their work.

- Have students facilitate small-group discussions of their work as a way to help refine their thinking.

- Plan for a congress discussion on the relationship between surface area and volume and on deepening students' understanding of the associative and commutative properties.

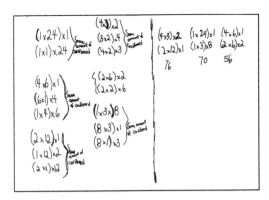

Figure 6

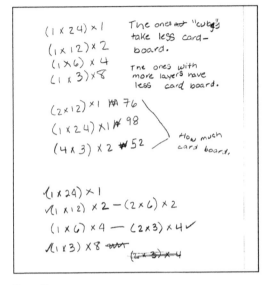

Figure 7

Tips for Structuring the Math Congress

Using your notes and observations made over the last two days, think about a structure for the math congress that will support students in further developing an understanding of the associative property, and the relationship between surface area and volume. To accomplish this goal, some teachers have found it helpful to select pieces of work that illustrate the following:

✦ An understanding of the congruency of the boxes. Students are able to articulate the "sameness" of a box with the dimensions $(3 \times 8) \times 1$ with boxes that have the dimensions $(3 \times 1) \times 8$ and $(8 \times 1) \times 3$. A sample like this gives you an opportunity to facilitate a discussion on how, when multiplying, factors can be grouped in various ways but the product remains the same (employing the associative and commutative properties). *[See Figure 6]*

✦ A clear explanation of why the box that is closest to being a cube requires the least amount of cardboard. A sample of work like this gives you a chance to facilitate a discussion on the relationship of the surface area to volume. *[See Figure 7]*

Facilitating the Math Congress

☀ As students share their strategies, encourage the class to generalize the relationship between surface area and volume.

Ask students to join you in the meeting area for a math congress. Have two or three groups share and invite discussion.

Inside One Classroom

A Portion of the Math Congress

Author's Notes

(The group that is sharing in this portion of the math congress is the final group to present.)

Max: Well, we started like everyone else. We had the different boxes for the 24 items and we found how much they cost and stuff. But what Joe and I are going to talk about is this. *(Points to writing on their poster.)* Here it says that we think the more cube-y boxes take less cardboard . . . so this one is cheaper. *(Holds up a $(3 \times 4) \times 2$ box.)*

continued on next page

Miki (the teacher)**:** Ooh, interesting word, *cube-y*. Can you talk to everyone about what you mean by the word *cube-y*?

Max: Cube-y is the opposite of long and thin. Cube-y is like this. *(Holds up the (3 × 4) × 2 box.)*

Joe: It's 3-D.

Max: Yeah, he said 3-D, but the way we first agreed on to describe it was *cube-y* so that's why we wrote it like that.

Miki: Why *cube-y* and not *cube*? What is the difference?

Max: If the box was a cube, the length and width and the number of layers would all be the same. All the sides of the box would have to be squares. We couldn't make that with the 24 cubes . . . this was the closest we could get . . . so we called it cube-y.

Miki: So you're saying that the more cube-y the box gets, the cheaper it is. Why do you think that happens?

Joe: Well, it's kind of like what Jeff and Maggie were saying before . . . about how when there's less showing it's . . . umm, wait *(looking for Jeff and Maggie's poster on the board)*, I think they were saying there's more, umm, what were you saying again?

Maggie: The boxes that show the least squares on the outside cost the least. The box that shows the most squares on the outside cost the most.

Joe: Right. So when it's like this *(holds up the (3 × 4) × 2 box)* there's more squares on the inside that's not showing. So you don't need cardboard for those. So it's cheaper.

Miki: OK, let's stop for a minute. This is a very neat point you're making here. Let's check in with the class to see if it's starting to make sense to everyone. Can someone restate what Max and Joe are talking about?

Chloe: I think you're saying that the box with the most squares showing is the most expensive because there's all those squares that are not covered. A long one, like that *(points to the (1 × 24) × 1 box that Miki is holding up)*, has a lot showing so you need more cardboard because there's more showing. But with that one *(points to the (3 × 4) × 2 box that Max is holding)*, there's less showing. Is that right?

Max: Yeah, so that's why if the box is cube-y, you know that there's more squares inside and you'll need less cardboard because you'll have less showing on the outside.

Miki: This is a pretty important point that you've noticed. Do you think that we can say, then, that the closer the box gets to a cube, the less cardboard is needed? For example, if you had 8 items, what do you think the dimensions of the cheapest box would be? Turn to a neighbor and share your thinking about this question.

Miki asks Max to elaborate on their newly coined term, "cube-y," since an understanding of its meaning is critical to grasping the main point of Max and Joe's conjecture. Developing a common language within a mathematical community is vital to communicating one's thinking effectively.

Miki questions Max and Joe further in order to develop this line of inquiry.

Terminology is clarified and the conjecture is put forth again.

Miki slows down the discussion at this point in order to assess the class's understanding of Max and Joe's work. She asks for a volunteer to paraphrase what Joe has just said.

Miki challenges her students to generalize, and asks them to consider a new problem.

Assessment Tips

The purpose of the math congress is to promote a discussion on several big ideas and strategies related to multiplication. It is also an ideal forum within which to observe and gauge students' levels of understanding as they share ideas, question each other, and defend and justify their work. During the math congress, you might ask yourself:

✦ Who is participating, and whom have I not heard from so far?

✦ Is this student able to restate what was just said?

✦ What kinds of questions are students asking?

✦ What connections are students making to each other's work?

Taking mental notes about students and using this knowledge to facilitate the congress is critical to helping students develop the mathematical big ideas and strategies that are the focus of the investigation. In addition to the dialogue taking place, the posters, recording sheets, and scrap paper (which lead up to the final written work) also serve as key assessment tools. Photocopies of significant work on scrap paper can be kept in your records (the originals should be kept in the students' math portfolios), and photographs of posters can be made as well. Take a look at the graphic of the landscape of learning (page 11). Do you have evidence that the big ideas and strategies shown there are developing? You may want to make a copy of the graphic for each student (to keep in your records on individual students) and shade in the big ideas and strategies you have evidence of thus far. In a sense, you will be mapping out students' developmental journeys as they work to develop a deep understanding of multiplication.

Reflections on the Day

Today students continued to work on the cardboard problem and created posters that depicted their work of the last two days. Sharing their work in small groups prior to the whole-class congress gave them an opportunity to refine their thinking about the problem. Discussion during the math congress led to a growing understanding of the relationship between surface area and volume, and a deeper grasp of the associative and commutative properties of multiplication.

Pricing Boxes

The day begins with a minilesson using a string of related problems to support the development of the strategy of doubling and halving. It then goes on to challenge students with tripling and thirding and the more generalized use of the associative property. A new investigation is then introduced in which students need to calculate the cost of several cubic boxes. During the math workshop on Day Five, students began to see that the cheapest box to make would be a cube. Today, students will work with three different-sized boxes: small ($2 \times 2 \times 2$), medium ($3 \times 3 \times 3$), and large ($4 \times 4 \times 4$). They will determine how many items each box holds and then figure out the cost of the packaging if the cardboard costs 12 cents per square unit. Students will also prepare posters showing their work, to be shared in the math congress on Day Seven.

Day Six Outline

Minilesson: A Multiplication String

* Work on a string of problems designed to encourage doubling and halving and tripling and thirding.

* Represent students' strategies on an open array (using graph paper arrays only if necessary).

Developing the Context

* Explain that today students will investigate the cost of three different cubic boxes and the number of items each box holds.

Supporting the Investigation

* As students investigate, engage them in discussions designed to highlight use of the associative property of multiplication.

* Ask students to make posters of their strategies for the math congress on Day Seven.

Materials Needed

Graph paper arrays, cut to match the problems in the minilesson (see page 42), and scissors, as needed

Cube boxes poster [If you do not have the full-color poster (available from Heinemann), you can use the smaller black-and-white version in Appendix C.]

Three boxes (rectangular prisms) built with connecting cubes: small ($2 \times 2 \times 2$), medium ($3 \times 3 \times 3$), and large ($4 \times 4 \times 4$)

Connecting cubes—one bin per group of two to four students

Drawing paper or graph paper (with squares that match the size of connecting cubes you have been using)—a few sheets per group of two to four students

Students' posters from Day Five

Scissors—one pair per group of two to four students

Large chart paper—one sheet per group of two to four students

Large chart pad and easel

Markers

Minilesson: A Multiplication String (10–15 minutes)

* Work on a string of problems designed to encourage doubling and halving and tripling and thirding.

* Represent students' strategies on an open array (using graph paper arrays only if necessary).

Today's mental math string encourages students to double and halve, but it then extends this strategy to tripling and thirding and the more generalized use of the associative property. Again, do one problem at a time, giving enough think time before you start the discussion. Today use precut graph paper arrays to support student strategies only if necessary. It is assumed at this point that students will be quite comfortable with the array. Model their strategies on the open array, and invite them to discuss the relationship between the problems within the string.

Behind the Numbers

The first three problems in the string are equivalent. The first two may remind students of the doubling and halving work they did in the minilesson on Day Two, but the third problem may provide some discussion. The first problem can be doubled and halved to reproduce it, but once solved it may also become apparent that the second problem was quartered and quadrupled. The next three problems invite students to consider other cases such as tripling and thirding. The big idea underlying the reason that these strategies work is the associative property: $(5 \times 3) \times 3 = 5 \times (3 \times 3)$. The last problem requires students to come up with their own helper problems. The numbers 24 and 3 have been used because students are quite familiar with the factors of 24 at this point. Thirding and tripling turns the problem into a fact they know: 8×9.

String of related problems:

6×8

12×4

3×16

5×9

15×3

45×1

24×3

Developing the Context

* Explain that today students will investigate the cost of three different cubic boxes and the number of items each box holds.

Display the cube boxes poster (or Appendix C) and the three rectangular prisms that you made with connecting cubes—2 × 2 × 2, 3 × 3 × 3, and 4 × 4 × 4—and then explain the following:

We've been doing a lot of work with designing boxes and coming up with cost-effective ways for a factory to construct them. Yesterday, during our math congress we talked about how less cardboard is needed the closer you get to a cube. This makes the cost less. So if we had 8 items, the cheapest box would be 2 by 2 by 2, like this [hold up the (2 × 2) × 2 box], where the length and width and the number of layers are all the same. Do you remember that? Can someone say more about that again?

Allow students to briefly discuss this observation from the congress on Day Five. Use the $2 \times 2 \times 2$ prism to illustrate this point, rearranging it if necessary.

> *Knowing that the cube is the cheapest box to make might be a real breakthrough for the box-making business! Now they can save money on cardboard by just making cube-shaped boxes. Imagine three cubic boxes: a small box, 2 x 2 x 2; a medium box, 3 x 3 x 3; and a large one, 4 x 4 x 4. I was wondering last night about this:*
>
> 1. *If we think about our connecting cubes each representing an item in the box, how many items fit in each box?*
> 2. *What would be the cost of each box?*
>
> *It turns out that the cost of making nice cardboard boxes, painted, decorated, and ready for items, is about 12 cents a square unit. For today's investigation, let's take a look at how much each box will cost to make and how many items each box holds.*

Have students use connecting cubes as a measurement unit and provide them with graph paper. Again, if you do not have graph paper that matches the size of the cubes you have been using then students can trace an outline of each box on blank paper and draw in the lines to make the square units. Give students an opportunity to restate the day's task and to ask questions for clarification before sending them off to work. Some students may already have an idea of how they want to begin, and this is a good time to have them share their thoughts.

Behind the Numbers

The numbers for this investigation have been chosen carefully to ensure that the associative property will get even more attention. Since the boxes are cubes, there will be six congruent faces (two-dimensional arrays) on each box. Some students will probably not make use of this fact; they will calculate the cost of each face separately and then multiply by six, or even use repeated addition. In either case, their strategy for the smallest box can be represented as (12 cents $\times 2 \times 2$) $\times 6$. Other students may work with the total surface area first. Their strategy can be represented as ($2 \times 2 \times 6$) $\times 12$ cents.

It is also likely that as students compare the 2×2, the 3×3, and the 4×4 faces, they will note some interesting patterns. The dimensions (width and length) are growing by only one each time, but the area grows quite differently. An L shape is formed around the initial square; thus the increase from a 2×2 to a 3×3 is 5 square units; from the 3×3 to the 4×4 it is 7 square units. Noting these patterns (made by the difference of consecutive squares) provides a new look at area, arrays, and dimensions. It also provides new insights related to volume. The number of cubes held by each box increases dramatically—from 8 to 27 to 64.

Supporting the Investigation

At this point in the unit, it is not unusual for students to be at varying developmental landmarks in their understanding of the big ideas and strategies related to multiplication. Some students may need more time and convincing to believe that the cube is the cheapest box to make. These students may go off on a tangent to continue to investigate this theory. Allow them the space to do so, but be sure to bring them back to the new investigation. Other students, who have yet to construct the associative property of multiplication, will probably need to use the cubes and graph paper to tackle this new investigation. Many students will struggle to see the relationship between surface area and volume as they determine the number of items in the different-sized boxes. These students will also benefit from using the cubes to build the boxes. Physically constructing the boxes is critical when supporting a range of learners.

☀ As students investigate, engage them in discussions designed to highlight use of the associative property of multiplication.

☀ Ask students to make posters of their strategies for the math congress on Day Seven.

This new investigation is designed to continue to support the development of the associative property of multiplication. As students work on the problems, here are some strategies you can expect to see:

✦ Working with each face one at a time, not realizing that all the faces on the cube are congruent. As you confer, encourage the students to record. As they begin to realize that each cube has six congruent faces, ask them if the groupings they use when they perform the multiplication can differ.

✦ Determining the areas of the faces, realizing there are six congruent faces on each box, and producing the following: $6 \times 4 \times 12$, $6 \times 9 \times 12$, and $6 \times 16 \times 12$. Now students are faced with some multiplication challenges. As you confer with these students, remind them of the work they did in today's minilesson. Encourage them to make the problems friendly and to group flexibly.

✦ Noting the increasing square and cubic patterns and becoming intrigued. Encourage this inquiry as you confer; it can become quite rich!

✦ Depending on your students' understanding of place value and money, you may need to address how the students' answers can be written to reflect the context of the problem. For example, if students calculate the cost of cardboard for a $2 \times 2 \times 2$ box as 12 (cost per square unit) $\times$ 6 (number of faces) $\times$ 4 (surface area of each face) $= 288$, how will this be written in the form of money? 288 cents? $2.88? Will your students know the difference between $2.88 and $28.80? Or even $288.00? Encourage them to consider the reasonableness of their answers. Stay grounded in the context and help them make use of their knowledge of money.

Students can work on this problem in their small groups from Days Four and Five. They should have access to their posters from Day Five to remind them of the strategies they used to find the cheapest and most expensive boxes. It is also a good opportunity for those still grappling with finding the cheapest box to revisit their work, and discuss in their groups why the cube requires the least amount of cardboard and therefore is the cheapest.

Today, you may see most of the students using cubes to build the boxes. It is not expected that students be familiar with the formula for volume, and do *not* give it to them. The contexts used over the next few days will help them generate it and the context will support students' ability to resolve their confusion. Allow them to build the boxes and calculate the number of cubes in their own way. Support their investigation by asking questions such as: Could you describe your strategy for figuring out the number of items? How did you use the connecting cubes to help you determine the number that fit? What do you notice about the number of cubes in this small box, the medium box, and the large box? Is there a more efficient way to figure out the number of cubes in a box? Invite students to make connections to the work they did earlier in this unit when they built boxes for 24 items. What do they notice about the number of layers and the dimensions of each layer, and their relationship to the total number of cubes?

You may also find that many more students are using the graph paper to help them figure out the cost of cardboard for each box. In this situation, there are more pieces of information to keep track of: the number of faces (sides of the box), the dimensions and surface area of each face, and the cost of the cardboard per square unit. For this reason, you may find a wider range of strategies. As the teacher, your goal is to continue to support your students in moving toward the horizon on the landscape of learning for multiplication (described on pages 6–9).

As you confer with the different groups, encourage them to articulate the strategies they are using and record them on posters for a gallery walk and math congress to be held on Day Seven. As the groups begin to create their posters, have them write down not only the number of cubes each box holds and the cost of cardboard for each box, but, more important, the strategies they used to derive the solutions. This will promote discussion of the strategies they used and challenge them to develop an efficient way to communicate their reasoning on their posters.

Inside One Classroom

Conferring with Students at Work (Chloe and Mary)

Author's Notes

Miki (the teacher): How's it going?

Chloe: Well, so far we figured out that there's 8 cubes in the small box since you already told us in the beginning. We're trying to figure out how many cubes fit in the medium-sized box.

Miki often enters into conversation with her students by simply asking how the work is going. The question invites an informal conversation on what the group has done so far, and it creates a level of comfort for students to share their developing ideas and, more important, their questions.

Miki: What strategies have you come up with so far?

Mary: I'm making the box right now so we can count the number of cubes. I've got 3 by 3 here *(holds up the 3 × 3 she made with the connecting cubes)*, and I just need to make 2 more.

Chloe: Wait, if you have 3 by 3, that's 3, 6, 9 *(counts by pointing to the rows)*, so it's 9 cubes, right? And then there's 3 layers altogether so that's . . . ummm . . .

One of the most important things a teacher can do is to ask questions that encourage students to articulate their strategy, and their thinking. Students who are not expected to share their thinking or are not used to the process will rarely do so on their own with other students. This is a skill that can be learned and must be practiced on an ongoing basis.

Mary: That's 27.

Miki: How did you get 27, Mary? That was pretty quick.

Mary: Because it's 9 times the 3 layers, and 9 × 3 = 27. So there's 27 items in the medium box.

Miki: So it looks like you were initially going to count the number of cubes in the medium box, but then Chloe noticed that you can just figure out how many are in each layer and multiply that by the number of layers. Is that right? Do you think we could always multiply the length times the width—what is in one layer—by the number of layers?

When Mary begins to share her thinking, Miki is explicit in the language that she uses, identifying specific strategies as more efficient than others. Efficiency is valued in doing mathematics.

Mary: Yeah, I think so.

Miki: Wow. That's pretty cool. That would be helpful to share in the math congress. Do you think you could find the number of cubes in the large box by using this strategy, which seems more efficient than counting each connecting cube?

Author's Notes

Michelle: Mei, how much cardboard do we need for the medium box? Did you make it? *(Referring to the cubes.)* Here, can you make the medium one like we did with the small one? Then we can figure out how much it costs.

Mei: *(Looking a little confused.)* Um, okay . . .

Miki *(the teacher)***:** Did you already figure out the cost of the small box?

Aaron: Yeah, it's 288.

Miki: But 288 what? Is it 288 dollars? That seems like a lot of money for a small cardboard box!

Aaron: No, no. I mean it's, uh, 288 cents. *(Talking to himself and trying to figure out how many dollars that is.)* That's $2.88.

Miki: How did you figure that?

Aaron: One dollar is a hundred cents.

Miki: OK, that makes more sense. I'd pay $2.88 for this cardboard box. So before you go on, can you tell me how you figured out that the small box costs $2.88?

Michelle: Well, we made the two things of 2 by 2 out of the cubes. And we put it together so that it was a cube. Then we counted the number of squares on each side.

Miki: Can I just slow you down right here? Can someone else tell me how you counted the squares on each side?

Aaron: Well, we didn't really count. We just knew it was 4 because each side was 2 by 2 and 2×2 is 4.

Miki: Mei, what do you think? Does that make sense?

Mei: Yeah. See this side? *(Pointing to one of the faces on the small box.)* There's 1, 2, 3, 4. *(Pointing to each square.)*

Miki: Good. It's also 2 across and 2 down *(pointing to one of the faces on the small box)*, which is the same thing as 2×2, which equals 4. Michelle, then what did you do?

Michelle: And then we knew there were 6 sides because we counted that on the small box, and we did 4×6 to figure out the number of squares.

continued on next page

Miki sees that the students have already found the cost for the small box, but have not generalized a strategy that might help them to be more efficient in finding the cost for the medium-sized box. She stops the group to help them reflect on their work so far.

Miki puts the problem back into the context by asking what the 288 represents. The context is critical in making sense of the answer.

Miki slows down the conversation to have the students clearly articulate their strategy for finding the cost of the small box.

Miki observed some confusion in Mei earlier and checks in with her.

Mei chose to count by ones, but Miki continues to push for efficiency in her students' computation.

continued from previous page

Miki: Aaron, so how many cardboard squares does the small box need?

Aaron: Ummm, it's 4 by 6, right? So it's 24 square units of cardboard. Then, we knew that each unit was 12 cents so we did 24 twelve times.

Miki: Wow, 12 × 24, that's a pretty big problem. How did you solve it?

Again, Miki slows down the conversation by asking the group to articulate their computation strategy for 12 x 24.

Michelle: Well, I know 12 × 12 because it's a multiplication fact. That's 144, and I just doubled it to 288 because 24 is double 12 so I doubled the answer too.

Miki: Wow, what an efficient strategy! That's great. Can someone else restate how Michelle solved 12 × 24 in your own words?

Miki acknowledges the efficiency of Michelle's doubling strategy and asks the group to restate it.

Mei: I think you said you doubled. And 24 is double 12 so you just have to double the answer and 144 + 144 is 288. Is that what you said, Michelle?

Michelle: Yeah.

Miki: Good work. So let me restate what your group did to figure out the cost for the small box. First, you did 2 × 2 to figure out the array on one side of the cube. Then you did 4 × 6 faces to figure out the number of cardboard squares on the surface of the small cube. *(Writes 4 × 6 on a piece of paper.)* Finally, you multiplied that answer by 12 cents, the cost per square. *(Writes × 12 next to the 4 × 6 so it is now 4 × 6 × 12.)* And that equals 288. *(Writes = 288 next to the equation.)* I wonder if you could apply this strategy to determine the cost of cardboard for the medium box. Do you think you'll need to build the medium box? What do you think?

Miki restates the strategy that the group used to determine the cost of cardboard for the small box. She writes the related multiplication problem on a piece of paper to explicitly illustrate their efficient strategy. This will also help them later as they apply this method to finding the cost for the medium box.

Mei: I think it might work, but we should still make the box to be sure.

Miki: OK, let's try it!

Reflections on the Day

Today you began a new investigation that continued to build on the students' previous work. On Day Five, students began to see that the cheapest box would be a cube. Using this new information, today's investigation revolved around two questions: how many connecting cubes fit in a small, medium, and large cube-shaped box, and what is the cost of the cardboard for each of these boxes if cardboard costs 12 cents per square unit? You may have seen many students using the connecting cubes and graph paper to work on this problem. Your focus today during the small-group conversations was to push the students toward generalizing a strategy in their work to further develop the associative property of multiplication. On Day Seven there will be a gallery walk, during which each group will have a chance to share their work, and then a math congress, in which specific groups will present their work.

Pricing Boxes

Materials Needed

Graph paper arrays, cut to match the problems in the minilesson (see page 49), and scissors, as needed

Students' posters from Day Six

Sticky notes—one pad per student

Connecting cubes— one bin

Large chart pad and easel

Markers

As on Day Six, today's work begins with a minilesson designed to support students' growing understanding and use of the associative and commutative properties of multiplication. After this minilesson, students will wrap up their investigation from Day Six and put the final touches on their posters. Each group will then have the opportunity to share their work during a gallery walk. This part of the investigation will conclude with two separate math congresses. The first, to be held at the end of today's math workshop, will focus on the development of the associative and commutative properties. The second congress will occur at the beginning of math workshop on Day Eight, and the focus of this briefer discussion will be on developing a general formula for calculating the number of items each box holds.

Day Seven Outline

Minilesson: A Multiplication String

* Work on a string of problems designed to support students' understanding and use of the associative property.

* Represent students' strategies on an open array (using graph paper arrays only if necessary).

Preparing for the Math Congress

* Conduct a gallery walk to give students a chance to review and comment on each other's posters.

* Plan for a congress discussion on students' strategies for determining the cost of each of the three boxes.

Facilitating the Math Congress

* Facilitate a discussion designed to generalize the associative and commutative properties by highlighting the different ways students have grouped and ordered factors.

Minilesson: A Multiplication String (10–15 minutes)

Today's minilesson reinforces the helpfulness of the associative property for computation when students group factors in clever ways. Again, introduce one problem at a time, giving enough think time for each before you start the discussion. Use the open array to model students' strategies and help students realize the meaning of what they are doing. If the open array does not appear sufficient, some students may benefit from still using precut graph paper arrays. Encourage students to share what they notice about the relationship between the problems, and facilitate discussion on the connections to the work they have been doing over the last several days.

※ Work on a string of problems designed to support students' understanding and use of the associative property.

※ Represent students' strategies on an open array (using graph paper arrays only if necessary).

String of related problems:

4×9

12×3

36×1

9×12

27×4

3×36

18×6

15×12

Preparing for the Math Congress

Provide students with time to put finishing touches on their posters if needed and then ask them to prepare for a gallery walk. Today's gallery walk will be similar to that of Day Three. Remind students that this is an opportunity for them to read each other's work prior to the math congress, and to comment and ask questions if anything is confusing or unclear. Encourage students to make connections to their own work. Pass out small pads of sticky notes and suggest that students use them to record their observations, questions, and the connections they see. They can place the sticky notes directly onto the posters. Give everyone about fifteen minutes to read and comment on the mathematics on the posters. Then allow a few minutes for students to read the comments and questions on their own posters. It is recommended that students write their names on the sticky notes. This allows students to respond directly to each other's comments, and reinforces the expectation that mathematicians share and discuss their work with each other in order to further their own understanding.

Behind the Numbers

Today's string begins with tripling and thirding, but the main focus of the string is the generalization of the associative property. The first three problems in the string are equivalent. Students may notice the tripling and thirding pattern readily here since it builds on their work from Day Six. The next four problems in the string are more challenging, each one pushing the students toward efficient computation. The 9×12 is a multiplication fact, although it may not yet be automatic. Students may use the partial products of 90 and 18, employing the distributive property. Tripling and thirding may be used to solve the three problems that follow. No matter what strategies are used, some students may begin to notice that $3 \times 36 = 3 \times (4 \times 9) = 4 \times (3 \times 9)$ and $18 \times 6 = (3 \times 6) \times 6 = 3 \times (6 \times 6)$. In order to solve the final problem in the string, students must come up with their own helper equivalent expressions. For example, students might try tripling and thirding right away, arriving at 5×36, based on their previous work. This may still be difficult for some to tackle without paper and pencil. Five, however, is always a friendly number to work with since it is half of ten. Using doubling and halving, the problem can be made quite friendly: $10 \times 18 = 180$. Students can also begin by tripling and thirding, which produces 45×4, and then doubling and halving to get $90 \times 2 = 180$.

※ Conduct a gallery walk to give students a chance to review and comment on each other's posters.

※ Plan for a congress discussion on students' strategies for determining the cost of each of the three boxes.

■ Tips for Structuring the Math Congress

Use the time during the gallery walk to make your final decision on who will share at today's congress. Review your notes and observations from the last two days, and think about a structure for the math congress that will support students in further developing an understanding of the associative and commutative properties. In selecting the students who will present their work today, choose students who have grouped factors differently so you can have a conversation on the commutative and associative properties. For example:

- Some students may not have realized initially that all the faces on a cube are congruent; thus they may have calculated the cost of each face first and then used repeated addition to calculate the total cost. For example, for the $4 \times 4 \times 4$ cube, they may have calculated one face as $(4 \times 4) \times 12$ cents. After figuring out this product, they may have added it six times to produce the total cost. Starting with a piece of work like this allows you to challenge the group to examine the congruency of the faces and to represent their strategy as $(12 \times 4 \times 4) \times 6$.

- Other students may have calculated the total surface area first and then multiplied by 12 cents. Their strategy can be represented as $(4 \times 4 \times 6) \times 12$.

These two strategies allow you to write the following equation for consideration in the congress: $(12 \times 4 \times 4) \times 6 = (4 \times 4 \times 6) \times 12$. Ask students to reflect on whether the grouping matters when multiplying (the associative property) or the order (the commutative property). Help students generalize these ideas. Next, examine a few of the ways students multiplied; for example, they may have hit roadblocks with the numbers at times: $4 \times 6 \times 12$ (small), $9 \times 6 \times 12$ (medium), and $16 \times 6 \times 12$ (large). These are large numbers. Did any students find clever ways to group the numbers in the calculations, reflecting strategies used in the minilessons you have been doing? For example, $4 \times 6 \times 12 = 24 \times 12 = 12 \times 12 \times 2 = 288$; $9 \times 6 \times 12 = 54 \times 12 = (54 \times 2) \times 6 = 108 \times 6 = 648$. The congress can conclude by examining how the associative and commutative properties can make multiplication easy and fun!

Facilitating the Math Congress

☀ Facilitate a discussion designed to generalize the associative and commutative properties by highlighting the different ways students have grouped and ordered factors.

Once students have had the opportunity to read the comments and questions written during the gallery walk, convene the class in the meeting area. Remind them that several groups will be presenting their work during this time and that everyone is expected to contribute by asking questions, making connections, and restating important information.

A Portion of the Math Congress

Author's Notes

Jordan: Brian and Mei are in my group, and we first counted the number of cardboard squares on the side of the cube for the small box. Like this. *(Shows how they counted by turning the 2 × 2 × 2 box each time to count the squares on each face.)* There are 4 squares. We multiplied by 12, so this side cost 48 cents. Then we counted the sides. There are 6. So we multiplied 48 by 6.

Miki (the teacher)**:** Any comments or questions for Jordan? Debbie?

Miki encourages students to comment and question each other. Implicitly she is saying, "We are a community of mathematicians. What do we think of this strategy?"

Debbie: I don't get that last part where you wrote 48 × 6 = 24 × 12. *(Points to the group's poster.)*

Mei: We halved the 48 and doubled the 6. We made it friendlier. Like the minilessons we have been doing. Doubling and halving. Do you get that?

Debbie: Oh, yeah. But then how did you do 24 × 12?

Mei: We knew 12 × 12 was 144. So then we doubled it.

Miki: Can someone restate how this group figured out the cost of cardboard for the small box?

By asking who can paraphrase, Miki is checking to see if everyone is following the conversation and understands the strategy being presented.

Max: Yeah, it's kind of how we did it in my group.

Miki: Max, could you come up with your group and talk about how your method is similar to Mei's group? *(Puts Max's group's poster up on the chalkboard.)*

Prior to the congress, Miki chose specific groups to share. However, she carefully weaves the discussion so that each group's presentation occurs naturally in order to maintain the flow of the conversation.

Max: We also knew that there were 4 squares on each side of the small box, but we didn't figure out the cost of one side first. That is what they did. We did 4 × 6 first. That was 24. And then we multiplied that by 12 just like they did, by doing 12 × 12 first and doubling it. So we got $2.88 for the cost of the little box, too.

Miki: Interesting. So let me write something for us to consider as a community of mathematicians. Jordan, Mei, and Brian, you did this, right? *(Writes:)*

$$(12 \times 2 \times 2) \times 6 = 48 \times 6 = 24 \times 12 = 2 \times (12 \times 12)$$

You figured out the cost of the cardboard on one side first; that's why I'm using the parentheses, because this is the part you did first. Then you multiplied by 6. Does this represent what you did? *(Students acknowledge agreement by nodding and so Miki continues).* And then, Max, your group did this. *(Writes:)*

$$12 \times (2 \times 2 \times 6) = 12 \times 24 = 2 \times (12 \times 12)$$

Miki highlights the use of parentheses in order to promote a discussion on the associative property.

continued on next page

continued from previous page

So the question I would like you to discuss is this: Does it make a difference what way we group when we multiply, or what order we do it in? Turn to the person next to you and talk about this. *(Allows time for pair talk.)* Debbie, what do you think?

Debbie: We decided it didn't matter. Max and Jordan sort of swapped . . . what they did . . . Jordan's group did the 12 first and Max's group did the 6 first . . . and it is also sort of like the minilessons we've been doing. You can make the problems friendly by making the groups be what you want. The numbers in what you wrote are just moving all around.

Miki: How many of you agree with what Debbie said? *(Students indicate agreement.)* This is pretty cool, isn't it? That we can make whatever groupings we want when we multiply . . . to make the work easier?

The associative and commutative properties are two very big ideas on the landscape of learning for multiplication. Miki provides time for pair talk in order to focus reflection on them.

▨ Assessment Tips

Anecdotal notes taken over the past two days during the minilessons and while the students worked in their small groups and in the math congress provide valuable insights into their learning, and into their present level of understanding. Ask yourself the following questions: What were their strategies for determining the price of each box? Did they count each square by ones, use repeated addition, or multiply? Did they realize that each face of the cube was congruent and that there were six faces? Did they double and halve when multiplying at times when it would be helpful? Have they generalized the associative and commutative properties? Such notes are critical in helping you plan future instruction to support students as they continue to explore multiplication.

Reflections on the Day

Today students continued to work on pricing the boxes, and finished posters that depicted their work over the last two days. The gallery walk allowed students to share their work, and to make comments on the work of others, prior to the math congress. This was an important opportunity for them to view each other's work critically and hold each other accountable for the written work. Finally, discussion during the math congress enabled students to make use of the strategies introduced during the minilessons within a real context, leading to a growing understanding of the associative and commutative properties of multiplication.

DAY EIGHT
Shipping Boxes

Today's math workshop begins with a brief congress on the box-pricing investigation. On Day Seven, students shared their ideas and strategies on how to find the cost of cardboard for each cubic box. The overarching goal for that discussion was to generalize the associative and commutative properties of multiplication. Today's poster presentations will focus on the strategies students used to determine the number of cubes that would fit in each of the three boxes. The structure of this congress is designed to develop a foundation for a general formula that can be used to determine the volume of each box. Students will then begin a new investigation that extends this understanding, as they attempt to pack first large (and then small) cubic boxes into a 4-foot-by-6-foot-by-4-foot shipping box for delivery to individual stores.

Day Eight Outline

Preparing for the Math Congress

* Plan to scaffold a congress discussion that will support students in generalizing a formula for calculating the total number of cubes in each box.

Facilitating the Math Congress

* Facilitate a discussion about the strategies students used to determine the number of cubes in each box.

Developing the Context

* Explain that today students will investigate how many cubic boxes can fit into a larger rectangular prism (a shipping box).
* Ask students to begin by exploring the larger (4" × 4" × 4") box first, as that will support their work with the smaller (2" × 2" × 2") box.

Supporting the Investigation

* Support students in determining the unit of measurement to be used for the investigation.
* Encourage students to generalize what happens when the box dimensions change.

Materials Needed

Students' posters from Day Seven

Before class, display these around the meeting area.

Packing poster [If you do not have the full-color poster (available from Heinemann), you can use the smaller black-and-white version in Appendix D.]

Masking tape

Two boxes (rectangular prisms) built out of one-inch wooden cubes: 2" x 2" x 2" and 4" x 4" x 4"

One-inch wooden cubes—one bin per group of three or four students

Calculator and ruler—one of each per group of three or four students

Large chart paper—one sheet per group of three or four students

Large chart pad and easel

Markers

Preparing for the Math Congress

☀ Plan to scaffold a congress discussion that will support students in generalizing a formula for calculating the total number of cubes in each box.

During the congress on Day Seven, students shared their strategies and ideas for figuring out the cost of cardboard for the small, medium, and large boxes. The structure of this congress allowed students to come to a generalization about the associative and commutative properties of multiplication. They discovered that neither the order nor the grouping of the factors changes the product. In today's math congress, students will revisit the box-pricing investigation with a focus on the strategies they used to determine the number of cubes in each box. This part of the congress will provide a foundation for the development of a general formula for volume—the focus of the subsequent investigation.

Convene students in the meeting area at the start of math workshop. Display the posters from Day Seven's congress on the chalkboard to remind students of the pricing investigation and the problems they have been working on over the last two days of the unit. Briefly review the big ideas that came up in the congress and invite students to articulate and restate them. Once you have completed a review of the congress on Day Seven, shift the conversation to the second problem in the pricing investigation—how many cubes fit in each box.

▨ Tips for Structuring the Math Congress

Review your notes and observations made during the last two days, and think about a structure for the math congress that will support students' gradual move toward a systematic approach to determining volume. In selecting students to present their work, choose posters that illustrate the following strategies:

✦ Some students may begin by building each box and counting the number of items in each layer. They may then add or multiply by the number of layers to find the total. This may mean that these students have yet to see the connection between the dimensions of the box and the total number of items it holds.

✦ Other students may not need to count. They may work more efficiently by realizing that the array in each layer can be multiplied by the number of layers to find the total; they are beginning to construct a working generalization of the number of rows × the number of columns × the number of layers for determining the total number of cubes.

Beginning the congress with a group that built each box and counted to determine the number of items may be more easily understood by all than beginning with a more abstract approach, such as multiplying the number of rows × the number of columns × the number of layers. Moreover, the discussion that would evolve from such an initial presentation would support succeeding presentations that involve a more systematic and generalized formula for determining the number of cubes. Plan on a discussion of the formula as the primary focus of the congress, though. Since the students' formula is about the number of cubes—not the cubic measurement of space in the box—the formula does not yet truly represent volume. In the investigation that will ensue after the congress, this formula will be generalized and extended to volume.

Facilitating the Math Congress

Convene a math congress in the meeting area and begin with a brief recap of the work from the math congress on Day Seven. Then shift the conversation to the second problem in the pricing investigation, which is: how many cubes are in each box? Invite the first group that you have chosen to the front, to discuss their poster.

☀ Facilitate a discussion about the strategies students used to determine the number of cubes in each box.

Inside One Classroom

A Portion of the Math Congress

Author's Notes

Miki (the teacher): Yesterday I had a conversation with Mary and Chloe as they were trying to figure out the number of cubes in the medium-size box. Mary and Chloe, could you come up and share your work with the class? *(Puts their poster up on the chalkboard.)*

Mary: Well, yesterday we were trying to figure out how many cubes there were in the medium box. We already knew that there were 8 in the small one since Miki told us at the beginning. We first made the box by making three 3×3 arrays out of the cubes and stacking them. *(Holds up the $3 \times 3 \times 3$ box.)*

Chloe: But then we saw that that's just 9 of the cubes 3 times. So we did 9, 18, ummm *(counting on fingers)*, 27.

Katie: Wait, where did you get the 9 from? I don't get that.

In a community of mathematicians, students are expected to openly ask questions without always being called on by the teacher.

Mary: The 9 is the number of items in each layer, and there's 3 layers so that's 9×3 and that's 27.

Miki: Chloe, I noticed that you counted by nine three times. What do you think about what Mary did, multiplying 9×3 layers and getting 27? Is that the same thing?

Chloe: Yeah, it's just faster.

Miki: So we can be more efficient by just multiplying 9×3 instead of counting by nine three times. Great! I notice that on your poster you did $4 \times 4 \times 4$ for the large box. Could you talk about that?

Mary: We just did the same thing that we did for the medium box. The 4×4 is each layer and then there's the 4 that's the number of layers.

Miki: I'm curious—did any other groups do something similar to Mary and Chloe by taking the length and width of one layer and multiplying it by the number of layers? Can we generalize this as a formula we can use?

Miki notices that Mary and Chloe were able to generalize a strategy for determining the number of items in a box. She articulates the strategy for the class to consider, and to determine if it can be generalized.

Assessment Tips

In addition to the anecdotal notes taken throughout this investigation and during the minilessons, the following questions may clarify what to look for while you observe and confer with individual students.

✦ What were their strategies for figuring out the number of cubes? Did they have to build each box or did they begin to see a pattern?

✦ How did they count each item or connecting cube? Did they count them one at a time or did they group them in certain ways?

✦ Is there evidence in their work that there was a gradual move from less efficient to more efficient ways of thinking about the problem?

✦ Have they generalized a formula for determining the total number of cubes?

Developing the Context

☀ Explain that today students will investigate how many cubic boxes can fit into a larger rectangular prism (a shipping box).

☀ Ask students to begin by exploring the larger (4" × 4" × 4") box first, as that will support their work with the smaller (2" × 2" × 2") box.

Display the packing poster (or Appendix D) and the two cubic boxes you built using the one-inch wooden cubes—a small (2" × 2" × 2") and a large (4" × 4" × 4"). On the floor in one corner of the classroom, use masking tape to mark out a rectangular area measuring 4 feet by 6 feet and also mark 4 feet up on the wall. This outline represents a shipping box with the dimensions (4 ft × 6 ft) × 4 ft. Explain the following:

We've been working with boxes for a long time now and I think we've become quite efficient box designers. We've also examined some pretty important questions regarding the cost of packaging. Did you know that a lot of companies that sell things that need to be packaged in boxes actually have an entire team just working on the best and cheapest way to package their product? It's a really important part of getting the items to the customer! Once the boxes are made and the items are placed in them, they are shipped to stores.

Display the 4" × 4" × 4" cube and explain that you have made a new box out of one-inch wooden cubes. Use a ruler and measure the width, length, and height and record 4" by 4" by 4." Ensure that you record using the word "by" rather than using the times sign. Today you are discussing dimensions—linear measurements—not the number of blocks. Then continue with the story.

Let's say that this 4-inch by 4-inch by 4-inch box is going to be shipped to a store. The best way to ship it is to pack as many as possible into a cardboard shipping box like this one I've outlined here. This particular shipping box is 4 feet by 6 feet on the bottom and 4 feet high.

Write on the board (4 feet by 6 feet) by 4 feet and then continue with the story.

Here's what I'm wondering:

- *How many of these 4-inch by 4-inch by 4-inch boxes will fit into this cardboard shipping box that is 4 feet by 6 feet by 4 feet?*
- *How many of a smaller 2-inch by 2-inch by 2-inch box would fit into the same shipping box?*

Students should begin this new investigation by exploring the large box first. Their work with the large box will support their exploration of the small box. Give students an opportunity to restate the day's task and to ask questions for clarification before sending them off to work. Some students may already have an idea of how they want to begin, and this is also a good time to have them share those thoughts.

Supporting the Investigation

Students can work on this new investigation in groups of three or four. With groups larger than four, it can be difficult for students to effectively share their ideas and ask questions. This activity requires students to move around and use math materials, which is also easier if the groups remain small.

Here are some strategies and struggles that you might encounter as you observe and confer with your students:

✦ You may see students beginning to build 4" by 4" by 4" prisms one at a time to fill up the shipping box. Do not allow this. Explain that there are not enough cubes to proceed that way, so the students will need to be more efficient in their work without actually making all the boxes. Ask them to predict how many boxes might fit. Encourage them to figure out how many will fit in just one layer, first.

✦ Some students may measure the outline of the shipping box with a ruler and calculate volume by multiplying length × width × height to produce 96 cubic feet. Next they may calculate 4" × 4" × 4" and get 64 cubic inches for the box. They may attempt to divide 96 by 64 and get a nonsensical answer of 1 remainder 32! As you confer, let them experience this disequilibrium, and then ask about the units they are working with. Once they realize that the units are not the same, they will be faced with how to turn 96 cubic feet into cubic inches. This conversion will provide quite a nice challenge that will force them into considering the type of unit that they are working with.

Behind the Numbers

The use of the small and large boxes and the dimensions of the shipping box have been chosen carefully to support the students' emerging understanding of volume. Do *not* provide enough cubes to allow students to build a shipping box out of them. Doing this would only be a counting activity. The fact that the dimensions of the shipping box are in feet, while the dimensions of the smaller wooden boxes are in inches, is purposeful. Students will be faced with the need to determine what the unit of measurement is: a cubic inch (one block) or the 4" × 4" × 4" box? Because the shipping box has a width of 4 feet and a length of 6 feet, one layer can be formed with a 12 by 18 array, or 216 boxes. Twelve layers fit for a total of 2592 boxes. The large box with the dimensions 4" × 4" × 4" requires eight times the volume of the small box with the dimensions 2" × 2" × 2". Each dimension of the 4" × 4" × 4" is double the dimension of the 2" × 2" × 2" and thus the number of small boxes that fit into the shipping box is 2^3 (or 8) × 2592. The dimensions of the shipping box are multiples of both 2 and 4, allowing students to work efficiently without getting bogged down by computation, and also enabling them to see patterns easily and try out strategies effectively. Allow calculators if needed, though. The point of the activity is to encourage students to examine how to measure volume (either in cubic boxes or cubic inches).

☀ Support students in determining the unit of measurement to be used for the investigation.

☀ Encourage students to generalize what happens when the box dimensions change.

✦ Some students may measure the outline with the 4" × 4" × 4" box. Since three boxes fit along every foot of linear distance, the measurement of the shipping box will be 12 × 18 × 12. The unit here is the cubic box (4" × 4" × 4"). Do not encourage these students to convert everything into cubic inches. This is a useful strategy because no conversion is needed. The question is, how many boxes fit? In the congress you will have an opportunity to discuss what the measurement unit is, and you can compare this to the unit used by those students who calculated volume in cubic inches. You can also support students to realize that the linear unit (4 inches) of the dimension when multiplied (L × W × H) produces a cubic unit of measurement—the 4" × 4" × 4" box and the unit if single inches are used is a cubic inch—one block.

✦ As students finish with the 4" × 4" × 4" box, they may attempt to use their results to calculate the 2" × 2" × 2" box. Encourage them to do so, because this will push them to examine what happens when the dimensions double—the new total is now the old total times 2^3—2 to the third power. They may, however, just double the quantity. Encourage them to examine just one layer and help them note the difference between that and the old layer. The new layer is the number in the old layer, times 2^2. Encourage students to examine this pattern and to generalize what happens when the dimensions change.

Inside One Classroom

Conferring with Students at Work

Author's Notes

(Ty and Michael have been trying to convert the dimensions, 4 feet by 6 feet by 4 feet into inches as Miki watches. Eventually they succeed).

Miki (the teacher)**:** So you have calculated the shipping box measurements in inches now. You have 48 inches by 72 inches by 48 inches. How does this help you to figure out how many of the 4 inch by 4 inch by 4 inch boxes fit? Michael, what do you think?

Often the best conferences begin from just watching and observing, then paraphrasing. This is what Miki does. And then she questions.

Michael: Well, there's 4 inches here. *(Places the box in the corner of the shipping box and points to the 4-inch length.)* It goes into 48 inches here 12 times. *(Points to the length of the shipping box)* And the width is 4 inches and that goes into 72 inches 18 times. So the bottom layer fits 12 × 18 boxes and that's . . . *(Writes 6 × 36.)*

Miki: I see you're trying out some of the strategies we've been discussing. Good thinking.

Miki compliments Michael on his use of the strategies they have been discussing, and then she supports him to consider others later. Mathematicians look to the numbers to decide on a strategy that is fitting, given those numbers.

Michael: 180 plus . . . 36 . . . 216 boxes. And it is 12 boxes high. I thought of it like the layers of items in the boxes we built last week. So then it's just 216 × 12. *(Starts to double and halve again.)*

continued on next page

continued from previous page

Miki: You could do that here again. But I wonder. Do you know
10 × 216?

Michael: Oh, yeah. That's a better way—2160.

Ty: And then just 2 × 216 more. That's . . . *(writes 432)* . . . so, 2592.

Miki: So you thought of the bottom layer first. The shipping box has
12 × 18 large boxes on the bottom and 12 layers so you calculated
it as (12 × 18) × 12? So how is figuring out the 4 × 4 × 4 box
going to help you with the small one?

Miki paraphrases the way that L x W x H can be used, and then she encourages the students to use what they know to calculate the number of small boxes.

Ty: Well, now we know that the shipping box is 48 × 72 × 48, and
we already know that the small box is 2 × 2 × 2. There's 24 small
boxes here *(points to the length of the shipping box)* because 2 goes into
48 twenty-four times and 36 here *(points to the width)* because 2 goes
into 72 thirty-six times and there's 24 layers because half of 48 is
24. So there's 24 × 36 on the bottom and 24 layers.

Miki: So now you're trying to calculate 24 × 36 × 24 *(writes this on
paper directly underneath (12 × 18) × 12)* to find the number of small
boxes that go in the shipping box? This is a tough problem. How
can we solve it?

By writing the two expressions near each other, Miki encourages the students to examine them together.

Michael: It's all double. See, 24 is double 12, 36 is double 18, and the
last 24 is double 12. I think you just have to double the answer.
(Uses calculator to multiply 2592 × 2.) So that's 5184.

Chloe: Wait, Ty and I got a different answer on the calculator. *(They have
multiplied 24 × 36 × 24.)* We got 20,736.

Miki: That's much more than Michael's answer. Michael mentioned that
there was a relationship between these two problems. *(Points to the
two problems on paper.)* What's going on here? Why doesn't doubling
work? Isn't this interesting?

Miki models the joy of inquiry.

Mei: Yeah. When we used doubling in other problems from the
minilessons, we just doubled one of the factors and then we
doubled the answer. That worked.

Miki: Hmmm. What a puzzle. What's doubled here? Each
factor doubled, right? If just one had doubled, what would
have happened?

Mei: That would make the answer double.

The use of the calculator allows students to check out their conjecture. But next they will need to examine the relationship, and prove it to the community.

Michael: It's double that and then double that again. That's 2 × 2 . . .
4 times . . . then times 2 again . . . 8 times.

Miki: Are you saying this big number, 20,736 is 8 times 2,592?
Check that out with the calculator.

Miki pushes the students to generalize and justify their thinking.

continued on next page

continued from previous page

Ty: *(Uses calculator.)* It is!

Miki: Why? Each dimension doubled and the number of boxes, when we measured with the little box, was 8 times more. Wouldn't it be nice to prove this? *(Writing on paper.)* So we did $(12 \times 2) \times (18 \times 2) \times (12 \times 2)$. Do you agree with that?

Ty: Umm, yeah. That's the same as $24 \times 36 \times 24$. Yeah.

Miki: And since we already know that we can move factors around in multiplication problems, could we also write $12 \times 18 \times 12 \times 2 \times 2 \times 2$ or $(12 \times 18 \times 12) \times 8$? What do you think?

Miki suggests grouping to remind them of the associative and commutative properties. Questions like this one challenge students to make generalizations that can form the basis for a mathematical proof.

Reflections on the Day

Today's math workshop began with another math congress on the pricing investigation. This initial discussion, focusing on the question of how many items were in each cubic box, supported students in generalizing a formula for calculating the total number of cubes in each box as a foundation for developing an understanding of volume. Today's new investigation provided an opportunity to generalize this formula further to the volume of a rectangular prism—in this context, the shipping box. The small cubic boxes with dimensions of an inch become a cubic measurement unit to fill three-dimensional space.

Shipping Boxes

The math workshop will begin with a minilesson that builds on the students' previous work with strings. Today's mental math string consists of related problems that continue to support the development and use of the associative and commutative properties of multiplication. Students will then have the opportunity to finish up their investigation from Day Eight, and to make posters of their work. The day's math workshop will conclude with a math congress in which specific groups will present their work from the shipping investigation. The discussion will focus on deepening their understanding of volume, and on coming to a generalization for determining volume.

Day Nine Outline

Minilesson: A Multiplication String

* Work on a string of problems designed to give students more experience in using the associative and commutative properties.

* Represent students' strategies on an open array.

Preparing for the Math Congress

* Ask students to make posters of their work and then conduct a gallery walk to give students a chance to review and comment on each other's posters.

Facilitating the Math Congress

* Facilitate a congress discussion on the units of measurement students used, the generalization of a formula for determining volume, and the relationship between the volume of each of the two cubic boxes.

Materials Needed

Packing poster (or Appendix D)

Two boxes (rectangular prisms) built out of one-inch wooden cubes: 2" × 2" × 2" and 4" × 4" × 4"

Students' posters from Day Eight

Sticky notes—one pad per student

Calculator—one per group of two or three students

Large chart pad and easel

Markers

Minilesson: A Multiplication String (10–15 minutes)

* Work on a string of problems designed to give students more experience in using the associative and commutative properties.

* Represent students' strategies on an open array.

This string is designed to reinforce realization of how helpful the associative property can be for computation, when students group factors in clever ways. Again, introduce one problem at a time, giving enough think time for each before you start the discussion. Use the open array to model student strategies and help students realize the meaning of what they are doing. Encourage students to share what they notice about the relationship between the problems, and facilitate discussion on the connections to the work they have been doing over the last several days.

Behind the Numbers

Today's string of related problems begins with two known facts that remind students of doubling. The second problem can be thought of as $(2 \times 3) \times 7 = 2 \times (3 \times 7)$, although most students will just know the answer. The third problem requires them to think of the relationship between 6 and 36. Many students may use partial products here ($30 \times 7 + 6 \times 7$); others may use the relationship between 6 and 36, i.e., $(6 \times 6) \times 7 = 6 \times (6 \times 7)$. The fourth problem is equivalent to the third, as one factor has doubled and the other has been halved. The last two problems build on a variety of the problems in the string. Encourage students to examine the relationships and to pull out factors to simplify the computation. For example, 56×36 is just $8 \times 7 \times 36$, and 7×36 has already been solved.

String of related problems:

3×7

6×7

36×7

18×14

28×18

56×36

Preparing for the Math Congress

* Ask students to make posters of their work and then conduct a gallery walk to give students a chance to review and comment on each other's posters.

Provide students with time to finish their work from Day Eight and to make posters for a math congress. Then explain that the class will have a gallery walk to give students an opportunity to look at each other's posters. Pass out small pads of sticky notes and suggest that students use them to record comments or questions, and then place them directly onto the posters. Give everyone about fifteen minutes to read and comment on the mathematics on the posters. Then give students a few minutes to read the comments and questions on their own posters. The purpose of the gallery walk today is to allow students to check answers and comment on each other's strategies. Because the numbers in this investigation are large, many students may have made calculation errors. If they see different answers in their classmates' work, they will need to reexamine their own work. Allow sufficient time for students to return to their own work if necessary.

▨ Tips for Structuring the Math Congress

The congress does not need to focus on the strategies students have used since these have probably been discussed during the gallery walk. Instead, think about how to structure the congress around three big ideas:

✦ the generalization of a formula for determining the volume of rectangular prisms

✦ units of measurement: the dimensions of the boxes are linear units of measurement whereas volume is measured in cubic units (either a cubic inch, a cubic foot, or a cubic box)

✦ the relationship between the small box (2" × 2" × 2") and the large box (4" × 4" × 4") in terms of volume—the dimensions of the box double but the volume of the larger box is 2^3 times the volume of the smaller box.

Choose posters that will encourage the community to discuss these three big ideas when selecting the groups that will present their work.

Facilitating the Math Congress

As you begin today's math congress, take a few minutes first to review the discussion from Day Eight's congress. This initial discussion of the general formula: (number of rows) × (number of of columns) × (number of layers), is critical in enabling students to make connections to their previous work, and in supporting the development of the big ideas and generalizations related to a general formula for volume in the shipping investigation.

☀ Facilitate a congress discussion on the units of measurement students used, the generalization of a formula for determining volume, and the relationship between the volume of each of the two cubic boxes.

A Portion of the Math Congress

Inside One Classroom

Author's Notes

Miki (the teacher): Carolina, your group figured out a great way to determine the number of boxes. You have a formula of length times width times height. Would you come up and tell us about it?

Carolina: Yeah, we measured with the box. The first layer was 12 × 18 and there were 12 layers altogether. So that's what we wrote here *(points to (12 × 18) × 12 on poster)* and we got 2592 large boxes. We thought it was like the items in the box when we did rows times columns times layers.

continued on next page

continued from previous page

Miki: And I saw that a lot of you used a strategy quite similar. Great work! Now I'd like Sam, Lisa, Tanisha, and Julie's group to present their work. I would like the rest of you to not only listen, but also try to see if you can find a connection between their work and Carolina's group.

Miki has a clear purpose here, and invites her students to be a part of it by asking them to find a connection between the presentations.

Tanisha: We also got 2592 boxes but in a different way. We knew that the large box is 4 × 4 × 4 and that equaled 64. And then we did the same for the shipping box that was 4 × 6 × 4, and we first got 96. But then we knew that was wrong because . . . ummm . . . *(Loses her train of thought.)*

Lisa: We divided and got 1 remainder 32. That would mean only one large box could fit inside the shipping box. Well, one box and a little bit more. And that's impossible because look at this box and the shipping box. *(Points to the display at the front of the room.)* You can see that a lot more than one would fit!

As mathematicians presenting their work to the community, students work together to explain what they did.

Tanisha: That's right. So then Sam said that we needed to change the feet into inches like the small box. So we did 48 × 72 × 48 and that's 165,888. We did that on the calculator.

Calculators can be very helpful here. They allow the calculations to be derived easily so the focus can remain on the relationships between the units, and on the generalization of a formula for volume.

Sam: And then we just had to figure out how many 64s were in 165,888. We used the calculator and got 2592.

Miki: Wow, that's a lot of big numbers on your poster and an interesting strategy. Let's take a minute to review their poster, and then I'd like someone to restate this strategy for figuring out the number of large boxes in the shipping box. Then we'll talk about how this is similar to or different from Carolina's group's work. *(Allows time for paraphrasing and discussion.)* So several of you have explained that each group used a formula of length times width times height. What I would like to discuss is what unit each group used.

Miki encourages paraphrasing to ensure that students understand the ideas of their peers.

Tanisha: I think their unit is the box, and ours was inches.

Miki: Hmmm. I'm a bit confused though, because isn't an inch just a line, like on the ruler? *(Holds up a ruler and points to an inch.)* How did this measurement tell you how many boxes fit?

Sam: It's like the little cubes. An inch by an inch by an inch.

Miki: So are you saying that an inch by an inch by an inch is like the shape of the one-inch cubes? Is it a cubic inch? Like a little tiny box?

Most students understand why L x W x H produced the volume. But what is the shape of the measurement unit? Miki knows this is a big idea for students to construct, and so she focuses conversation on it.

Carolina: Oh, I get it. It's like you tried to find out how many little inch boxes were inside the 4 by 4 by 4!

continued on next page

64 THE BOX FACTORY

continued from previous page

Miki: So how many of the little inch boxes are in the 2 by 2 by 2 box? Let's see . . . the width is double, the height is double, and the length is double. And then the 4 by 4 by 4 is double the width and double the height and double the length of the 2 by 2 by 2. I'm going to write this down and then I would like you to form groups of three and discuss how these units are related.

$1 \times 1 \times 1$	$2 \times 2 \times 2$	$4 \times 4 \times 4$
1 cubic inch	8 cubic inches	64 cubic inches

By making a chart of the data and staying with just the small boxes and the cubic inch, Miki creates a focus on the relationship between an increase in dimension, and its effect on volume.

Reflections on the Day

In the minilesson today, students were encouraged to make use of the associative and commutative properties as they continued to work on efficient computation for multiplication. In the math congress, they worked to generalize a formula for finding the volume of rectangular prisms, and they examined the characteristics of the units used for measurement, and the resultant effect on the volume when each dimension doubles.

A Day for Reflecting

Materials Needed

Large butcher paper for the wall display (eight feet long or more depending on available space)

Students' work from throughout the unit

Drawing paper—a few sheets per student

Scissors and tape

Markers

In today's math workshop, students create a learning wall. To create this community wall, students revisit all their work from the past nine days, retracing their thinking and charting the big ideas, strategies, and models that they examined in their investigations. Questions that were raised but left unexplored are posted on this wall as possible future explorations for the mathematical community.

Day Ten Outline

☀ Work with students to create a wall display to highlight the work they have done throughout the unit.

Building the Wall Display

Gather the students in the meeting area. Have them sit next to their math partners. Begin by telling students that you are going to document all the work they have done over the past nine days. This document, called a learning wall, will be placed in the hallway (or some other prominent place in the school) as a record of their mathematical explorations and ideas. This learning wall will have two purposes. First, it will allow students to revisit all their work and think about what they have learned and what questions they may still have. These questions might become the basis of future explorations. Second, since the learning wall will be placed outside the classroom, the rest of the school community can also think about their ideas. Emphasize that this is a document of *their* learning. And because it is a public document, it needs to clearly communicate the scope of their learning.

As part of creating this learning wall, ask students to revisit all their work from the past nine days. To support them in this task, it might be helpful to make a list of the various questions they explored. Post the first question they explored and ask students to examine their work and think about what important ideas came up during this discussion. As a classroom community, choose several pieces of student work that are representative of the big ideas and strategies that came up in the math congress. Also post questions that arose during this discussion. Any questions that have not yet been explored can be listed under a heading like "Our Questions for Future Exploration."

There are many ways to create a learning wall. The primary purpose is to give students an opportunity to reflect on their own thinking, and then to consider how their ideas fit into and contribute to the mathematical learning of the entire classroom community. It is also a way to emphasize the role that communication plays in mathematical life. It is one thing for students to communicate their ideas to a math partner and then to share them within the classroom community. It is quite another to communicate these ideas to a larger community. Doing so requires students to sift through their work and think about what is important, and how they want to communicate these ideas. Students cannot do this without self-reflection, which is one of the critical tools for them to develop as learners.

The main goal here is to create a *living* document that accurately reflects your students' experiences in this unit and that invites passersby to interact and post comments and ideas as well. There should be samples of students' work that exemplify their strategies, struggles, and questions. Although the class is creating the learning wall as a community, the final document should be organized by you in a way that clearly communicates students' development. Here are three big ideas to keep in mind as you organize this material:

- What were the questions that students explored? These should be clearly delineated and be representative of the progression of the unit.

- What did students learn? Find pieces of work that clearly represent the ideas developed by the classroom community.

- What questions were raised? Some of these questions have been answered; others may still need to be explored. This should be indicated on the document.

> ☀ Work with students to create a wall display to highlight the work they have done throughout the unit.

Assessment Tips

After the learning wall has been created, ask students to reflect in writing on what they learned during the past two weeks. Ask them to trace their thinking by choosing an idea they started with. Examine with them how and why this idea changed. This written reflection can then be placed in their math portfolios.

Reflections on the Unit

The mathematician Samuel Karlin once said, "The purpose of models is not to fit the data but to sharpen the questions." In this unit, the three-dimensional array was used as a model to represent multiplication, specifically to explore the associative property. This model was developed through a number of different problems, all connected to the context of boxes. Students also used two-dimensional arrays to explore the relationship between the surface area and volume of rectangular prisms. Eventually, in the shipping box investigation, students developed a general formula for volume and examined a variety of measurement units and the relationship between the doubling of dimensions and the resulting changes in volume.

Minilessons in the unit supported students toward efficient calculation for multiplication, specifically making use of the associative and commutative properties for multiplication. The *Contexts for Learning Mathematics* unit *Minilessons for Extending Multiplication and Division* in this series can be a helpful resource for further exploration of these ideas and strategies.

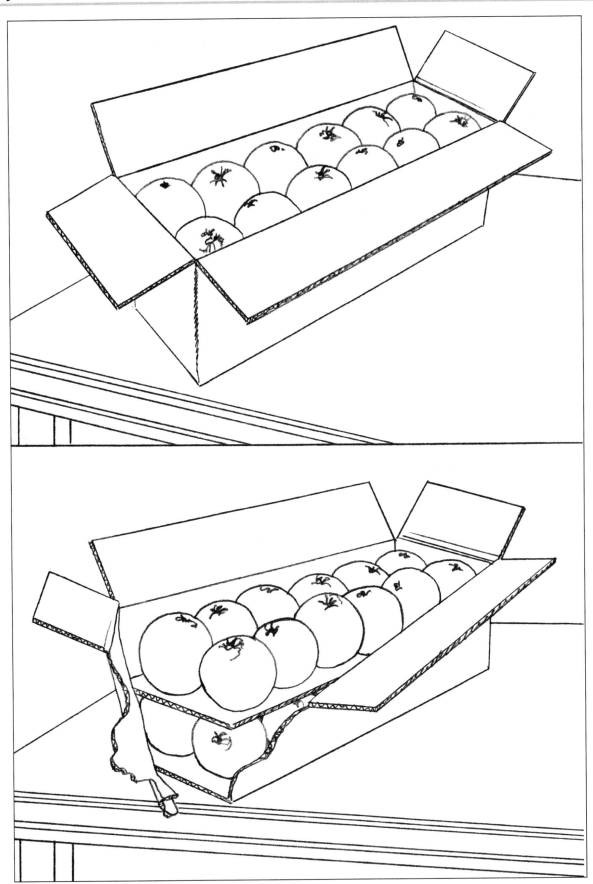

Names _____ Date _____

Here are 16 possible box designs. How much cardboard is needed for each?

Box Design	Square Units of Cardboard Needed
$(1 \times 24) \times 1$	
$(2 \times 12) \times 1$	
$(4 \times 6) \times 1$	
$(8 \times 3) \times 1$	
$(2 \times 6) \times 2$	
$(4 \times 3) \times 2$	
$(1 \times 12) \times 2$	
$(8 \times 1) \times 3$	
$(4 \times 2) \times 3$	
$(2 \times 3) \times 4$	
$(1 \times 6) \times 4$	
$(2 \times 2) \times 6$	
$(1 \times 4) \times 6$	
$(3 \times 1) \times 8$	
$(1 \times 2) \times 12$	
$(1 \times 1) \times 24$